PRAISE FOR *A BRAIN THAT BREATHES*

'A kind, calm, warm book. Reading it feels like taking a deep breath.'
JESSICA STANLEY, author of *Consider Yourself Kissed*

'Jodi's warm and intimate writing delivers sharp, current science to create a masterwork of living with intention. If you want to understand your brain, learn to rest and enjoy life, read this brilliant book now.'
RACHAEL MOGAN MCINTOSH, author of *Mothering Heights*

'I am someone who has pushed myself to near burnout too frequently and for too long. I was a little nervous to read Jodi's book, as I didn't think I had the capacity to make the changes I needed to. However, I'm so glad I did because the strategies she suggests are accessible, achievable, and they truly work. After initiating some small changes and strategies, I can see the benefits – and I now feel hopeful that it's possible to step back from near burnout, rather than overwhelmed that it's not. Thank you, Jodi, for writing the book I needed to read.'
DR ELIZA HANNAM, GP

'A gentle, thoroughly researched book filled with quiet wisdom. Using powerful evidence, Jodi shows us true wellness begins with the brain.'
INDIRA NAIDOO, author of *The Space Between the Stars*

'Blending lived experience with psychological insight, this book is both reassuring and refreshingly human. With compassion and clarity, it offers a quietly radical alternative to quick-fix self-help'.
MILLIE HARDIE, psychologist

'Jodi Wilson is a crusader for a simpler life, pushing back at a world that shouts at us to be more, to do more, to spend more. She celebrates the power of doing nothing and taking back our attention to find moments of stillness in our too-busy lives. *A Brain That Breathes* is a practical guide to dialling down the intensity of modern life.'
MAGGIE MACKELLAR, author of *Graft*

'I simply adored this wise and generous book. In *A Brain that Breathes*, Jodi gently and compassionately explores ways of being that are fundamental not just to our mental and physical health but to our very humanity. It offers practical building blocks for a more present, calm and contented existence that isn't about perfection but about meaningful change amid the beautiful mess of our lives. This is a balm of a book, and essential reading for our uncertain times – an antidote to doomscrolling and anxiety. I felt calmer and more present just reading Jodi's words. This is a book that will quietly transform lives.'
MIRANDA LUBY, author of *The Edge of Everything*

'Jodi Wilson is a modern guide for body and mind. With equal parts science, heart, and common sense, *A Brain That Breathes* offers a luminous road map back to ourselves, showing us how to find the safe haven we each long for, not through grasping or escape, but within the ordinary rhythms of everyday life. I can't think of anyone who wouldn't benefit from reading this brilliant book.'
RACHEL SAMSON, clinical psychologist and co-author of *Beyond Difficult*

'Jodi Wilson's words never fail to calm and illuminate. In *A Brain That Breathes*, she combines a compassionate voice with deep research to help you slow down, breathe and make space amid the uncertainties and clutter of daily life.'
KATE MILDENHALL, author of *The Hiding Place*

'A call to, and celebration of, a more mindful, intentional life. Reading this was like curling up with a cup of tea and letting a deep, over-stressed breath out. It's exactly what I needed to read.'
SARAH AYOUB, author of *The Yearbook Committee*

'If success these days is a calm nervous system, then this book shows you how to get there. With each chapter, my breathing deepened. I think this is the book we should pick up each day as a reminder of how we can move through life with ease.'
LAEL STONE, educator, speaker and author of *Your Own Story*

A Brain That Breathes

This book was written on
Tommeginne Country, the unceded
lands of the Palawa people –
the original storytellers.

A Brain That Breathes

Jodi Wilson

Essential habits for an overwhelming world

What our brains really need to be happy, healthy & productive

murdoch books

Sydney | London

Published in 2026 by Murdoch Books, an imprint of Allen & Unwin

Murdoch Books Australia
Cammeraygal Country
83 Alexander Street,
Crows Nest NSW 2065
Phone: +61 (0)2 8425 0100
murdochbooks.com.au
info@murdochbooks.com.au

Murdoch Books UK
Ormond House, 26–27 Boswell Street,
London WC1N 3JZ
Phone: +44 (0) 20 8785 5995
murdochbooks.co.uk
info@murdochbooks.co.uk

 A catalogue record for this book is available from the National Library of Australia

A catalogue record for this book is available from the British Library

ISBN 978 1 76150 080 0

Cover design by Laura Thomas
Text design by Kristy Allen
Typeset by Midland Typesetters, Australia
Printed and bound by CPI (UK) Ltd, Croydon CR0 4YY

Murdoch Books acknowledges the Traditional Owners of the Country on which we live and work. We pay our respects to all Aboriginal and Torres Strait Islander Elders, past and present.

EU Authorised Representative: Easy Access System Europe, Mustamäe tee 50, 10621 Tallinn, Estonia, gpsr.requests@easproject.com

10 9 8 7 6 5 4 3 2

 The paper in this book is FSC® certified. FSC® promotes environmentally responsible, socially beneficial and economically viable management of the world's forests.

Contents

Some keep the Sabbath going to Church –
I keep it, staying at Home –

Emily Dickinson

I have done nothing all summer but wait for myself
to be myself again.

Georgia O'Keeffe

Loosen, loosen, baby
You don't have to carry
The weight of the world in your muscles and bones
Let go, let go, let go

Aly Halpert

For Mum and Dad

prologue

I live on an island at the bottom of the world, and each day I walk
the coastline, lifting my face to the sky and inhaling deep lungfuls
of air – salty, cold clarity. At Cape Grim, the north-westernmost
point of the Lutruwita/Tasmania mainland, the southerly wind that
pummels the ragged coastline is the purest air in the world. When
that wind travels east, it curls around the small coastal town I call
home. It is expansive and unfiltered, and it lets the light through
without the gauze of pollution. I dream of bottling it, this most
ordinary and precious of things.

I write most days at a desk in the corner of my living room.
During school hours I type and read, the fire burns, the dog
sits at my feet. I settled in this small town after travelling in a
caravan for more than two years with my partner and our four
children. We sold most of what we owned so we could live a
little lighter, without clutter or obligations. We intentionally
created space so we could spend time with our kids before their
childhood evaporated. Some may call it running away, but I see it
more as a huge leap to the side: we hopped off the conveyor belt
and figured out our own path.

Eight years on, a shift first to van life – and eventually island
life – remains one of the best decisions we've made. Living in

a small space without a schedule immediately shrank the scale of my attention, and my new-found presence amplified my distraction of the years before. This was most pertinent when we were remote and off-grid, our days slow and centred around ancient habits – consciously using water and food (nothing was wasted), cooking over a fire, exploring new landscapes, napping under trees, stargazing. Packed tight and cosy in our home on wheels, we lived with only the essentials and learnt that you don't need a lot to live well. And so we wondered: what *do* you need to live well? And on the flipside, how can we let go of the unnecessary?

I'm still asking these questions. I worry each day about inconsequential things. My energy spirals upwards and I ground myself with deep breaths. I'm charmed by ordinary things. I busy myself with words and books and wish the hours didn't pass so quickly. I think – perhaps too much – about how nice it will be to get into bed at night, preferably with tea and a hot water bottle. I am easily distracted by my phone and I feel deeply uncomfortable at the ease with which I pick it up and become immediately transfixed. I want to be curious about life. I read investigative journalism features and feel bereft at the hard, hard lives so many millions of people live while I exist in almost constant comfort. I intentionally seek breathing space each day, even when deadlines are looming and the mess of the family home feels chaotic. I revel in the challenge of my work and thrive on productivity, but I also know it can easily push me to exhaustion if I let it. I'm learning to recognise the heady spiral of too much work and too little space. When I'm grasping for answers and letting everything else go, I know I need to step back.

Most days begin the same way: I walk or write for an hour and then coax children from their beds. I fry eggs, make coffee and pack lunchboxes. The dog nuzzles between the kitchen bench and my leg in the hope she'll catch a stray piece of ham. It is a busy, noisy hour of dressing and eating and searching for whatever is lost (a sock, a shoe, a book) until the children walk out into the cold, closing the front door and leaving me in the quiet. The bookend to the day is the same level of busyness and chatter before I lie in bed and listen to the sounds of settling: a bed creaks, a page turns, the light switches off. A morning and night poignant in their ordinariness. When success is framed as rapture, normality is left lacklustre. And yet if you live it, you know it to be the root of contentment. Happiness exists here if we slow down long enough to notice.

When people come to know about my life on the road, the most common question I'm asked is how have you held on to the lessons you learnt? But what they're really asking is how have you prevented your life from filling back up again?

Life did feel unsustainable for a while there, so I started 2024 with the intention to carry less – stuff, pressure, obligation – and create space. It didn't feel like a big deal at the time, but it led me down a scientific path that helped me better understand my brain and what it needs to be creative and productive. It didn't take me long to realise what now seems so obvious: in an artificial, hyper-convenient world, we're always looking for the next quick fix. But the long-lasting changes we crave are the simple habits our ancestors practised every day.

I could have enrolled in a vipassana meditation retreat in the name of research, but what I really wanted to learn was how I could make room for the things that matter in my very ordinary, everyday life. I wanted to explore how we can create this space by ourselves, without having to leave behind what's normal and necessary. I think this is how we can ensure it isn't a luxury – an 'other' – and instead make it practical, actionable and accessible. Uncertain times always bring us back to what matters. And sometimes it prompts a mindset shift that leads to a sense of hope, despite everything.

I knew I wanted to move through my days feeling less restricted. No matter how busy work and family life was, I wanted to make sure there were gaps between the doing. This meant I had time to do what felt intuitively right in the moment and had the strong mindset to protect it, knowing that many things could wait. I also wanted to know *why* we find it so hard to find breathing space and, on the flipside, how we can benefit when we do create moments of intentional pause in our day.

I went looking for the science to counterbalance the onslaught of often saccharine self-help tips that pepper socials, and what I found was rather simple: we don't need help, we need basic human care. It's not complicated, either. Instead of looking ahead for answers, we need to consider age-old essential habits – the simple practices that slow us down, encourage us to breathe and ground us in the moment (ideally on the grass and in the dirt). In a world focused on self-improvement, where we're always encouraged to 'be our best self', I just wanted to become more aware, to get to know who I am and what I need so the bright ideas keep coming, so the words flow.

I was charmed and comforted by what I learnt. Life tumbles on, but I don't feel so rushed now.

Introduction

Like a chorus carried from one person to the next, 'It's a lot,' we say. And then sometimes, 'It's just too much.' This is how we describe modern life with its 24-hour consistency.

For so long now we've been lured by the promise of bigger and better, a paradigm that requires more energy than most of us have to spare. We've been conditioned to look ahead and chase, craving what we don't have and clinging to what comes next, a cycle of dissatisfaction that emphasises what we fear most: uncertainty.

When it all feels like too much, the brain pulls back and the mind muddles, often when it's least convenient.

You may know this numbness, this exhaustion like a stubborn weariness that settles in the bones. It's understandable that so many of us feel this way. We've been conditioned to optimise every hour of every day and, despite the niggles and doubts, we keep going – ignoring the tiredness and pushing through. The body responds in the best way it knows how: by focusing only on what is essential. It shuts down so it can hone its attention on what is vital in the moment – sleep and rest to strengthen the systems that are frayed. The body is a force of nature; it almost always gets its way.

A sense of unravelling may be normal, but it's also making us unwell, as evidenced in increasing rates of burnout and mental illness. And when we reach the point of feeling like we don't care or we can't be bothered, the most prolific advice is usually to *prioritise self-care*, which sounds just like another to-do – obligatory work that requires even more effort, organisation and funds. *Where do I even start?* you may think.

The roots of self-care as a concept are meaningful. It originated as an attentive form of care to ensure strength and vitality for Black feminist activists. But like most things of value, its true meaning was lost as self-care became swept up in capitalist rhetoric: *Buy this and do this and eventually you'll be better!* There's a fine line between self-care and self-improvement, which comes disguised as another productivity hack to optimise our 'best self'. It's also deeply embedded in tech: instead of listening in, we're conditioned to watch the numbers and chart our commitment, letting the data dictate how we feel. On top of that, it's a multitrillion-dollar global industry.

No one is making any money when we choose to rest, do less and immerse ourselves in nature. But a quieter life isn't something we need to earn. Science tells us it's actually what we all need for longevity. Productivity isn't a dirty word, but there's only one way to achieve it and also maintain physical and emotional equilibrium. We need to return to ancient habits that counterbalance modern expectations and obligations. They were the scaffolding of daily life for most of our evolutionary history, always supporting our wellbeing. They can support us now, too – they let the brain breathe.

The most meaningful of life practices aren't particularly bright new ideas, they are age-old habits that bolster us in the confusion and chaos of hyper-convenient, AI-assisted modern living. They remind us how to be human. Yes, you may consider them overly simplistic, but that's precisely why they're vital: they're biologically necessary for us all. When we prioritise them, we're creating a really strong foundation for wellbeing. These habits are essentially small steps back to what's most fundamental to our existence – our humanity.

This looks slightly different for each of us. You may need active rest: intentionally breaking from work, savouring small moments of stillness, letting your mind wander, seeking comfort. If you are neurodivergent or have been diagnosed with mental illness, medication may be the foundation on which to build those habits. For most of us, being in conversation with someone who, as the Benedictines say, 'listens with the ear of the heart' provides the stillness we need to pause and, eventually, regulate. When we slow down, we experience a rerouting of sorts that often prompts questions about what really matters in life – what's working and what's not?

Our brain needs a break because they weren't designed to be used constantly while we sit immobile for most of every day. Instead, we evolved to use our bodies and our hands and to follow the most essential habits: to live according to the seasons; to seek sunlight for regulation; to honour rest to restore immune function and emotional regulation; to eat for energy and vitality; and to move to release tension and build strength and stability. We are cyclical creatures and our energy is dictated by internal and external seasons. This is basic biology, and it always has and always will require us to create intentional breathing space between the producing, creating and making – the busyness and fullness of life.

On the surface these seem like frivolous practices – what we do on the rare occasions we have great swathes of time stretching out in front of us. But here's the thing: they are scientifically proven to be mentally and physically bolstering. And that's precisely what we all need right now: evidence-based proof of what sustainable care actually looks like.

Through honouring these elements of basic care, our aim is to create breathing space each day in our ordinary lives. We all know what this is: moments of pause and reflection, a period of rest and retreat; the antidote to busyness and burnout; the opportunity to slow down, meander and observe regardless of the fact that there are many things on the to-do list that are still undone. What we know about all the essential practices that allow us this breathing space is that they don't require excess time or resources. In this sense they're accessible to all of us. It's not about looking out for answers but compartmentalising our day – taking breaks, prioritising downtime, intentionally turning away from screens – and returning to our basic human needs. Every day we should do something that we would have been doing 10,000 years ago: bask in a patch of sun; take a mid-afternoon nap; breathe deeply while looking out at the horizon; sit under a tree and have a bit of a think. This is how we get back to basics. And often we only heed the call of the body when it starts to shout obnoxiously at us with pain, lack of energy or the undeniable shift of ageing as we enter a new phase and are humbled by its life-altering reality.

This book is about acknowledging the fortifying benefits of breathing space for the brain and the body by putting these simple, essential habits into practice. They singularly support our resolve, creativity and productivity, which gives us room to breathe even when life feels pressing – *especially* when life feels pressing.

———

After the publication of my first book, I started to share
a weekly list on Instagram titled 'Five ways to practise
simplicity'. A few readers reached out to say *my* story resonated
deeply with them, but they also wanted practical tips for
applying simplicity to their *own* lives. I soon realised that
writing a list each week was actually a tiny act of care – for me
and for my readers. It became a ritual where I sat and thought
most about what I needed for the week ahead. And so many
people would respond with, 'I don't know how you always
seem to suggest what I need!' But here we are, all living in the
world and navigating all the hard and ordinary stuff that makes
life beautiful and challenging. Of course we all need the same
reminders for how to live well. Sometimes just a little reminder.

So what are the practical steps to finding breathing space
in a world that feels like it's continually picking up pace, that's
growing increasingly noisy with demands and rhetoric that
just feel like *too much*? This question informed my unofficial
'project' as I sought to better understand my brain. It wasn't
a radical undertaking; it was small and quiet, invisible even –
a gradual learning that slowly shifted my thinking and,
subsequently, my awareness. I didn't need to change my life
to find breathing space in my days. It was already there. I just
needed to pay attention.

I was encouraged and motivated by research that examined
the health benefits of intentional space for a settled nervous
system and for a brain that has the opportunity to wander and
light up with solutions instead of being crushed into numbness
by excess stuff. I realised that this is exactly what's happening
to all of us as we're busily caught up in a growth myth that
never has and never will revere our humanness.

This is the undercurrent of all our lives, the belief that continuous economic growth is vital even though it is detrimental to our environmental and social wellbeing. We're all carrying the weight of 'more' and it's heavy and debilitating. This is why we feel stuck.

And so I developed a more careful noticing of how I was feeling, and a greater confidence in what I needed in the moment. And with time, I started to restore my attention and live with more intention and less distraction. I didn't need to overhaul my life to do this and neither will you. But you may need to switch your thinking and slow down long enough to ask yourself: *What do I need?* And that naturally leads to: *How do I want to feel?*

This, I realised, is something I could change in the moment by getting offline and going outside, by resting for 10 minutes instead of pushing through mind-numbing tiredness, by swapping half an hour at the desk for a gentle stroll. This is how I started to feel like I had a brain that could breathe, and with time I started to feel more like myself, more human.

I decided to view everything that was familiar to me through a different lens – one informed by what I had learnt about the brain and the (offline, analogue) life it was designed for. I realised that we spend so much time thinking we need self-care when we could be using that time to be quiet and still and give our brain what it really needs – a break from the relentless barrage of contentious information and mind-numbing entertainment.

I want to live a creative life – I want to be productive – but I'm also a partner and a mother of four, with a mortgage on a small house that contains too many odd socks and a long list of unfinished jobs. Life is full but it doesn't mean my brain needs to be. I realised that when I feel overwhelmed, my brain is telling me that there's no space left. The remedy is simple: put the phone down, let my mind wander, resist distraction and spend time outside. This is how we mentally declutter and create breathing space in the mind.

———

Of course, we exist in a dopamine culture where we chase the feel-good chemical released when we scroll on our devices. But even the man who invented the infinite scroll – Aza Raskin – later regretted it. He admits that if we don't give our brain time to catch up with our impulses, we just keep scrolling. When we pick up our phone, we enter what's known as a ludic loop – a repeated cycle of uncertainty, anticipation and feedback. These unpredictable, feel-good rewards across all social media platforms are just enough to keep us going. They entice us to habitually pick up our phone and keep scrolling. Our lives are defined by how we spend our time and what we pay attention to. Time is the most ancient human currency, and in modern life it feels like it's slipping away because we're distracted. We're no longer aware of the value of minutes and hours, so of course we feel like there's no time to do what makes us happy.

Perhaps you just want to get off your phone and be in your own life, look up and out so you catch the tiny morsels of joy that exist all around you and allow them to move through you. Sometimes it feels like a small moment of happiness. Sometimes it feels like magic.

But how can we protect these moments so they don't evaporate, slip through our fingers, fill up with demanding items of importance? Awareness helps. Intention, too. Mostly it's practice, because when you start to access breathing space – in your home, in the garden, while walking slowly down the street – you'll start to *feel* in your body what it is, and with time this makes you think, act and choose differently. These habits are *essential*. It's not so much an intellectual experience as a primal one.

With this understanding comes the incentive to tune in to your body and take heed, to accept that breathing space isn't something you need to earn; rather, it's the foundation of a slow and intentional life free from idealistic expectations and urgency. Breathing space is the fundamental work required to create and produce.

If you're here reading this, you care somewhat about slowing down and simplifying, perhaps living with less so you can create more time for yourself. Maybe you want to make your life more beautiful in tiny, meaningful ways, leaning in to rituals of reverence and celebration so you can foster a deeper connection to the natural world and its seasons. Through untangling and picking apart what we've been conditioned to think is necessary, we naturally progress to the point where we ask: *What is too much?* And perhaps more pertinently: *What is enough?*

This isn't about being enough or doing enough. It's about flipping the narrative and asking yourself what is enough for you right now. And where you can find a bit of space – uncover it, dig around for it, carve it out.

In each chapter you'll find simple, actionable suggestions so you can take what you learn and apply it – wherever you are and however you live. It's all well and good to nod to the benefit of slowing down, but in a world where so many are struggling and our concerns about life and the earth become increasingly prominent, choosing to go slow is a privilege. And yet, as psychologist Dr Lara Bertolino says, it's also a requirement of being human.

We can push against our innate needs as much as we like, but it doesn't change the fact that every cell in our body requires habitual and sustained periods of rest for longevity. We are essentially cutting our life short if we don't create breathing space for ourselves and each other.

When we spend our days longing and searching for great swathes of time, we skip over the small moments that offer our brain space to breathe in the middle of things. But we can remind ourselves that the parts of our days that are mostly unremarkable in their mundanity are the guiding lights when we become overwhelmed and stuck.

There's never anywhere else to be than right here.

That's why right here is a really good place to start.

This isn't about working out what to do with your life; it's an invitation to find a bit of space today, and then tomorrow, and maybe even as far ahead as next week.

How do you start?

Subtract one thing.

What Do We

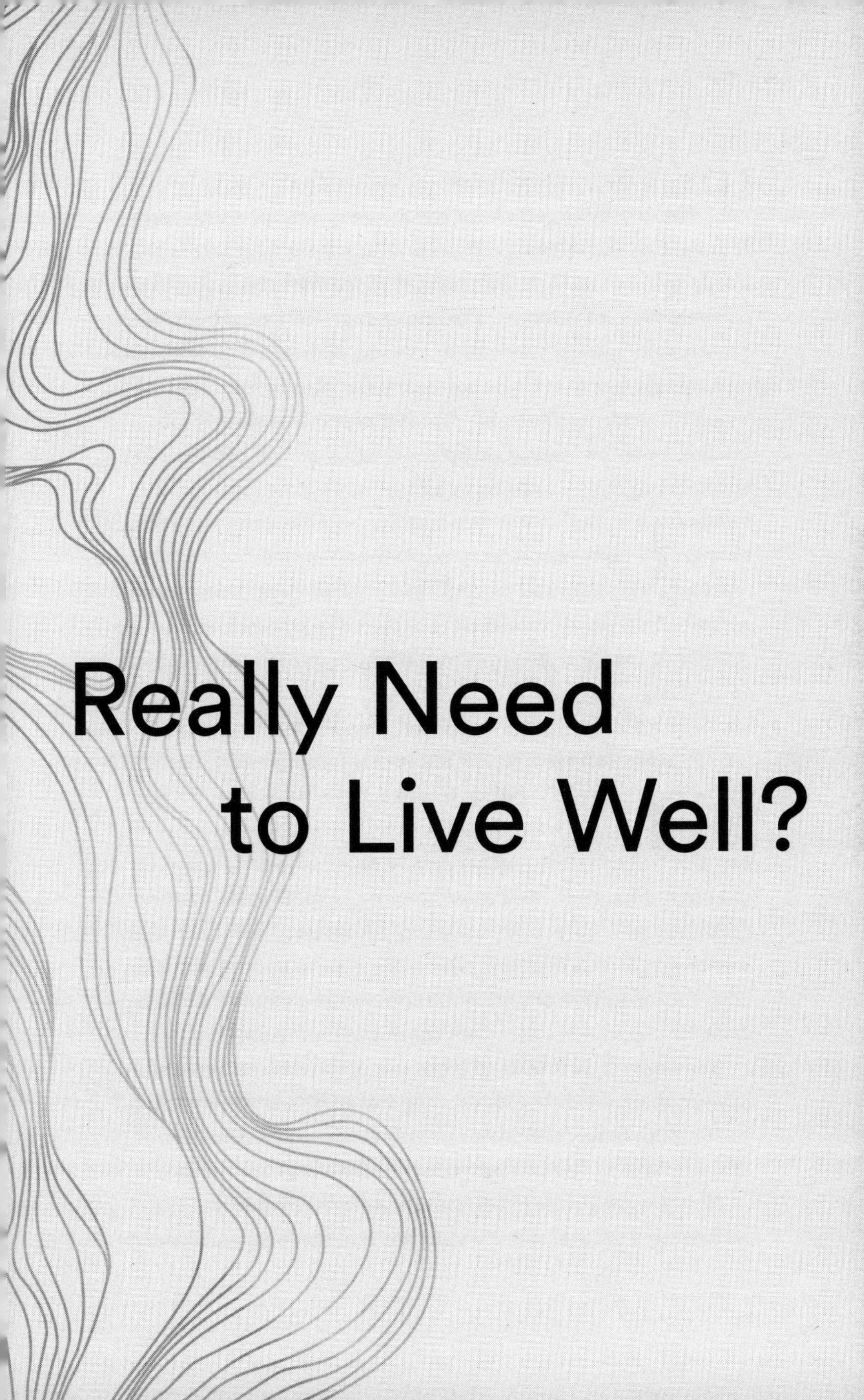

Really Need
to Live Well?

This is the question we all ask but we don't always have the energy to search for the answers. It's for this reason that we find ourselves scrolling to distract ourselves from the heady spiral of modern life, further exacerbating our feelings of unease and discomfort. Making change feels hard because it requires the mental capacity to foresee, plan and decide. And on any normal day, that's a bit too much for many of us, especially when life is already full and demanding. So let's simplify it: what if we focus instead on creating a tiny pocket of breathing space in our days – one day at a time? This most essential of habits fits seamlessly into modern life because it doesn't require change, it simply requires us to pause and notice.

Neuroscientists and psychologists define breathing space as 'soft'. 'Soft fascination' refers to the calm state when our mind is at ease and free to wander, where our attention can gently move from one thing to the next. It's the mental state we slip into when we are in nature, where our attention isn't harnessed by sensory stimuli but gently fascinated by them: the sway of a tree, the falling of a leaf, the ebbing tide. It's like downtime for our brain, which is why it is such a powerful practice for everyone, but especially those who are engaged in hours of focused, hard attention on a regular basis. Nature doesn't require direct attention but allows us to move through it with a lightness of being, which creates the opportunity for both self-reflection and mental reprieve. The results? Mental decluttering, clearer thoughts, more aha moments.

You know how it feels to focus intently: you lean forward in your chair, your shoulders creep towards your ears, you hold your mouth firmly shut, your breath exists only in the canopy of your chest as you furrow your brow and curl your spine.

Now I want you to think about how it *feels* when you are walking in a natural space – your garden, the local park, along a riverbank or the rocky outcrop of the coastline. Your gaze is gently – ever so softly – wandering from one thing to another as you set one foot in front of the other. And as you do, your whole body softens.

Breathing space is a period of intentional rest. In the world's largest 'Rest Test' survey, the things most likely to promote deep rest were solitary acts: walking, swimming, reading. Essentially, we need to be alone to recharge, but that doesn't mean we need to retreat from normal life to do so. Intuitively we know how good we feel when we sink into a fluid yoga practice, sit in meditation or prayer, walk through green space or swim in the ocean. But this feeling – that we're taking care of ourselves – is backed by science. And the benefits are profound: we are rejuvenated at a cellular level, which protects us against the biological processes of ageing.

In her poem 'Fire', Judy Brown writes:

> *What makes a fire burn,*
> *is space between the logs,*
> *a breathing space.*

If you feel like you've misplaced your verve for life, perhaps breathing space will help restore it. Intentional space is fuel for living.

You may not feel very useful in moments of rest, but rest gives you what you need to move forward – perspective, energy, mental clarity. This matters because, as the years pass, you want to be standing and in good working order, with the ability to make choices and, if you feel inclined, make change. Wherever you are, however you live, there is the work of every day – the labour of life, the deadlines and appointments, the washing and cleaning and organising; the odd socks, the missing Tupperware lids, the cluttered wardrobe, putting food in the fridge, getting meals on the table, tending to the people around you, caring for yourself.

It's for all these reasons that breathing space can feel unattainable, because you're right: there's always something you could be doing, a person who needs you, an email to respond to, a job to complete. You may feel a ghostly disapproval if you stop and do nothing. And that's why you need to start thinking about breathing space as *something*. It's a significant something, too – it's the proven antidote to stress.

———

You've stopped to read this sentence. If you read this one and the one after it, you'll begin to come into stillness. In stillness there is space, because instead of moving and grasping, you are suspended, attentive only to the page. With each breath and each paragraph you relax: physical tension relieves and your heart rate slows.

If you choose to put this book down for a moment, look up from the page to gaze into the middle distance, or close your eyes and consider what you've read – let yourself be with the words and the thoughts that emerge, without having to explain or even make complete sense of them. You're experiencing what the Japanese call yutori – space in the mind. All things have more than one name.

Poet Naomi Shihab Nye calls this 'living in a poem': 'When you think, when you're in a very quiet place, when you're remembering, when you're savouring an image, when you're allowing your mind to calmly leap from one thought to another, that's a poem. That's what a poem does.'

Perhaps it's idealistic, but it's not a stretch of the imagination to consider a lifespan in stanzas, unfurling slowly before they pick up pace – a rush and a run – and then retreat to the finality of a full stop.

We live in stanzas, life seasons. A life is a poem.

Research shows that the brain – more specifically the hippocampus – segments each day into chapters, a neurological filing system that actively organises our experiences according to meaning based on what we care about and what we're paying attention to. The details we notice influence each new chapter in our life story, the one that is noted and stored in our memory like a script. In our truest form, we are creatures searching for meaning, and our memories are ordered accordingly.

Where do we search for meaning? We've been conditioned to look for it in achievement, and so the central question to life becomes: 'How can I be most productive today?' And because we're hurrying through the hours, chasing what's ahead and documenting it along the way, we often don't stop long enough to realise that what we've got now is what we once wished for.

In adulthood (and increasingly in childhood), there are fewer moments for quiet contemplation because we've been taught – trained! – to stay busy, make plans, reach goals and grasp for the next opportunity. If there is open space in front of us, we dive in to claim it. We are always trying to make the most of things, to maximise our time and optimise ourselves. It's rare to let something be.

We are a society of doers – the ancient habits of waiting and wandering are no longer essential so we've effectively removed them from our lives. And so we're missing the mental benefits of these mellow states. Individually and collectively we have a yearning for space:

> **space** *to breathe and be without abrasive distractions*
> **space** *to think without questions being asked*
> **space** *to move without judgement of the body*
> **space** *to create without the ideals of perfection*
> **space** *to feel safe so we can settle and rest.*

Perhaps you've thought to yourself: *I don't want to live like this any more.* But then you get stuck, because what are the next steps? And do you have the mental capacity to consider them and then put them into practice? Or do you feel like so many of us do: that you can't possibly make another decision right now?

Breathing space doesn't exist ahead of time. It's there when you slow down and tether yourself in the moment. And that doesn't mean living a slow life per se, but slowing down when you walk in the door and put your keys in the bowl. A breath, because you've got a home to come back to ... A breath when you're brewing your morning coffee, because this is a moment to savour, not one to rush past ... A breath when you're making a decision or starting a hard conversation or about to embark on something you're resisting ... A breath, because life will always contain some hard stuff and this is the 'work' ... A breath when you're cradling your baby while your child tugs on your skirt, your eyes are heavy and the house is a mess, because exhaustion and love, grief and magic are all tied up in a single day.

I'm not here to tell you that slow living is better or easy or the only way. But I do know that you can live a somewhat slower life and still be quietly ambitious, still *live big*. I know because I live it. My work can be busy and I can be productive, but I can step away from the desk and life is immediately slowed – because of where I live, yes, but also because it's a conscious choice I've made. Some may look at my life and frown on the lack of restaurant dinners, the few social plans, my unabashed love of an early night, the smallness of it. But that's just how I like it. In psychology it's known as both/and – you can have a fast, full, brimming life and still have space to breathe. And perhaps that space – the ability to be grounded – is what's most crucial to productivity, because when we feel settled and not stressed, the answers come, the solutions are obvious and creative stuck points untangle. And sometimes that space, however mediocre it may seem, is enough, just as it is.

For a writer it looks like time away from the page instead of 1000 words every day. For a doctor it's altering one person's experience through a minute of compassionate care instead of making sweeping systemic change. For a gardener it's recognising that the soil that grew a glut of juicy tomatoes one year needs a fallow period in which to rest, and yet often the basil and rocket and cherry tomatoes will self-seed and the fruit you never planted will grow regardless.

In the West we tend to think in binary terms of either/or – *Can't have it all!* – but both/and is a way of life in Japan, where this dialectical thinking requires a certain level of discernment. The origin of the word discernment is sieve, and I like this visual: to maintain what matters and let everything else fall away, subtracting what you can. Writer Annie Dillard refers to habits as 'a net for catching days' – the reliable scaffolding we need when life feels particularly uncertain.

Life *is* inherently uncertain, which is why we find immense comfort in routine and why making momentous change feels *too big*. Breathing space is simpler than that. Consider it a seam in the patchwork of your days. It's learning that what needs untangling in the mind often requires handiwork in the form of building or washing dishes or even walking on uneven surfaces. It's celebrating the opportunity for a nap – even a short one –

and recognising it as tangible care, not abject laziness. It's about being preoccupied, perhaps even enchanted, by ordinary things – summer stone fruits, swollen spring buds, the low light of a log fire. If you want to attend to your life, to create some breathing space, you start by attending to the everyday. Japanese author Haruki Murakami refers to these tiny morsels of joy, in his essay 'Afternoon in the Islets of Langerhans', as 'a small but certain happiness'. When they collect and compound over days and years? I think that's contentment.

A calm nervous system

The nervous system was designed for humans who lived in the moment, not those who are always accessible, logged on and thinking ahead.

If your body is your home, it is also a lighthouse; it gives you warning signals so you can seek safety. This internally wired alarm system is normal human biology – we are designed to experience and withstand stress because it moves and motivates us.

Psychologist Dr Lara Bertolino considers it helpful to compare our evolutionary past with modern life because it simply explains how far we've drifted from the world we were designed for. The cavernous gap between our reality then and our reality now helps explain so many afflictions. 'If you think about how our bodies were designed – we are hunters and gatherers; we were designed to have brief periods of high-intensity activity and longer periods of pottering around, shooting the breeze, chatting while collecting, sitting around the fire sharing stories for hours on end. We lived in small communities and our awareness was focused primarily on the moment – who we were with and what we were doing. Yes, we experienced moments that were really high-pressure and stressful: running from a threat or chasing something to hunt it. But the threats weren't consistent. We weren't designed to sit at a desk for nine hours a day and then sit in the car on the way home and feel the conceived threat of many things, all over the world, often all at once.'

Safety is what we instinctively search for from the moment we're born. A newborn finds it from their birth mother, who is considered to be the baby's 'habitat' – she is a safe house, as are our other caregivers until we have developed the cognitive and emotional ability to stabilise our stress. The part of the brain responsible for this regulation and impulse control is the prefrontal cortex, and it takes 25 years to reach maturation. Our primal urge to feel safe persists through life. When we're emotionally safe, we experience a sense of comfort and ease; we feel like we've come home. We all crave this feeling, especially during periods of profound stress. We sometimes refer to it as 'breathing space', but if we use the lens of the nervous system, it would be 'safe space'.

STRESS AND THE AUTONOMIC NERVOUS SYSTEM

The sympathetic and parasympathetic nervous systems are parts of the autonomic nervous system (ANS) that have opposite but complementary roles:

- **The sympathetic nervous system** *carries signals that put the body on alert in response to threats.*
- **The parasympathetic nervous system** *carries signals to relax, restoring the body to a calm and composed state, and preventing it from overworking.*

They work together to maintain balance in the body – consider it the body's protective mechanism. It's evident from birth when a newborn seeks the warmth and touch of their mother for safety and survival. For as long as we live it remains, controlling the unconscious processes of breathing and digestion, influencing our decision-making and informing our health and wellbeing. The way we live can either exacerbate or dampen the sympathetic (stress) or parasympathetic (calm) systems. The way most of us live means we're in an almost constant state of stress. The ideal is an even keel between 'fight or flight' and 'rest and digest'. You don't want your sympathetic nervous system to be constantly activated, but you don't want it to be inactive either; it's a survival mechanism that is on alert for danger.

I was curious about our baseline state as humans. Are we hardwired to be stressed or at ease? According to generalised unsafety theory of stress – or GUTS, an acronym that charmingly nods to the place we often feel our fear – our baseline state is one of anxiety and stress, where we seek safety signals to feel settled. Prolonged stress isn't always a result of life stressors but about feeling unsafe.

Generalised unsafety is also an evolutionary survival mechanism, which is why it's typically more prevalent in people who are experiencing some level of disturbance to their equilibrium, such as:

- *loneliness – now a public health concern with a physical impact equivalent to smoking 15 cigarettes a day*
- *low social status and fatigue*
- *inability to access natural spaces*
- *stressful working environments.*

I'm not sure of the exact details of your life, but we do know that the chronic stress of modern life stems, in part, from its ambiguity and our connection to everything that's going on in the world. When we can predict what's coming next and we are concerned only with our small community, we feel safer – the brain loves predictability. And yet as renowned Buddhist teacher Pema Chödrön says, 'Uncertainty is all we have.'

So much of the stress we carry around could be filed under 'uncertainty stress', and most of us find this deeply uncomfortable. But there are people who are comfortable with uncertainty. It's a rare quality of resilience but, as psychologist Dr Elissa Epel says, it is something we can learn. File it under 'control the controllable': the more you practise, the more habitual it becomes.

DEVELOPING RESILIENCE TO UNCERTAINTY

The human brain thrives on certainty and control, and yet modern life forces us to navigate uncertainty and essentially get comfortable in the discomfort of not knowing. How can we balance this unavoidable stress and still live well?

Our bodies are designed to survive – no matter our situation or circumstance. Our DNA becomes modified in subtle ways throughout life, particularly in response to traumatic events, when epigenetic molecules attach themselves to our genetic code and switch some genes on or off. From an evolutionary perspective, this means that our bodies are designed to withstand the trauma we carry – from our own experiences and also from the trauma inherited from our parents and grandparents. This is called 'epigenetic inheritance'; within our cells, we carry the stories and, in part, the stress and uncertainty of our ancestors. These stories inform our survival mechanism – the 'fight or flight' response that kicks in to protect us in stressful situations. We react not just to our circumstances today, but to all the stories we genetically carry as well.

The way we perceive stress also determines how we feel about it. This is why some people don't consider uncertainty to be stressful. While the scientific theory may be new, the concept isn't. It's the hallmark of Buddhism and yogic practices: life is impermanent, all we know is this moment. Be here now; for now, just be here.

The simple method over the page is perhaps the best place to start if you want to find some stillness and stability, despite the uncertainty. Think of it as respite, consider what it is in its most basic form: care.

Stop. Breathe. Be.
This simple, quick brain-reset technique can help
you slow down in the moment and foster a mind–
body connection. With practice, it rewires your
brain so you feel less stress.

1. **Stop** whatever you're doing – consider it an
   intentional pause in your day.
2. **Breathe** slowly and deeply – let out a few sighs if
   it feels good.
3. **Be** – it can help to close your eyes and become
   aware of how you're feeling.

There's no right or wrong way to do this. If you
want to be here a bit longer, shift your weight slowly
from one foot to the other and then press firmly
into both feet, grounding yourself.

WHAT STRESS DOES TO THE BODY

Our cells require a certain level of optimisation to function
as they should, which means they can go through their
natural processes that keep our immune system working
and our energy levels at a prime. Cellular stress occurs when
the body lacks proper nutrition or adequate sleep, and it's
exacerbated by environmental pollutants, chronic stress and
emotional trauma.

The body reads all of the things that have become normal in
modern life as stressful, which is why many of us are stuck in
'fight or flight'. The *vagus nerve* is the body's communication
pathway. When the body is experiencing chronic stress, the

vagus nerve tells the immune system that something is wrong and it needs to be on guard.

The nervous system interprets stress as a threat, and this directly affects cellular function, which ultimately pulls us out of homeostasis (physiological steadiness or equilibrium) and becomes the root cause of illness. This subsequently leads to brain fog, exhaustion, irritability, impulsive behaviour, depression, anxiety, disease – the maladies that slow us down in order to protect us.

Genetics informs our stress and our stress response. Everyone's experience of the same stressors is different. And yet we all innately know the difference between the heart-racing immediacy of adrenaline (a stress hormone) and the gooey, cosy warmth of oxytocin (the love hormone that flows when we experience comfort and safety). Stress is a hormonal experience, so when we focus on the physiological power of hormones, we can begin to understand how to counteract the stress hormones cortisol and adrenaline with feel-good chemicals that benefit and bolster our mood, energy, motivation and perspective.

The ANS functions like a tug-of-war between two subsystems:

1. **our activation (sympathetic nervous) system** – *alert, vigilant, at the ready*
2. **our rest (parasympathetic nervous) system** – *easeful, laid-back, relaxed.*

Daily life for most of us is stressful, which is why many of us experience sympathetic nervous system dominance; it's the stronger side. But that doesn't mean we can't actively strengthen our parasympathetic nervous system. In fact, it's absolutely possible with awareness and practice (see Training your vagus nerve, page 86).

The sympathetic nervous system responds to fear by sending blood to the muscles, increasing breathing rate and heart rate, and releasing glucose into the bloodstream, giving us the energy and alertness to flee. This is why it's called the 'fight or flight' response: we need a quick release of energy to achieve both. It's why many of us thrive when we're close to a deadline: the energy rush gets us to the finish line and then we collapse, mentally frazzled and physically exhausted.

But modern stress is also worn as a badge of honour. If we're stressed we're also busy – we're working, we're successful, we're powering ahead. And yet stress inhibits mental clarity. In small doses it can help us be productive, but any more than that and it's destructive – to our short-term mental efficiency and our long-term cellular vitality. We are at our least efficient and effective when we're stressed because our body is focused on *running from danger* rather than thinking rationally, intuitively or creatively. High cortisol is also associated with an increase in negative thinking and lower quality of life because it creates a significant amount of inflammation in the body and affects it on every level – the lines on our skin, the way we breathe and move and digest, our energy and perception, how much we *care*, right down to our organs and cells. This can mean lowered longevity, weight gain, strokes and high blood pressure caused by elevated levels of cholesterol in the system.

This type of stress is known as *di*stress. You may even experience the sense of being stuck and unable to make decisions; this is known as the 'freeze' state. Freeze actually comes on board after fight and flight have been activated, so while it may be more dominant, they are all present.

When stress is good for us

Stress isn't all bad. We need stress to be enthused and motivated. A life without stress would be stagnant and lacklustre. Stress can push us along and ensure we're focused and paying attention.

This 'good' stress is known as *eustress*. It's commonly referred to as beneficial stress because it increases our focus and performance, and provides us with a sense of fulfilment by moving us towards an outcome. Ultimately, it helps us meet challenges and experience the satisfaction of achievement, progressing from *I can't do this!* to *I **can** do this!* When the challenge is exhilarating and we approach it with alertness and focus rather than panic and fear, we may even enter a state of *flow* – a period of mental focus where the answers come easily and we ride the wave of easeful productivity.

Any creative knows the feeling of being in flow, the delicious effortless space where time expands and it seems as though some magic is at play. The ease can make us giddy as we try to hold ourselves there – not grasping but suspended – the tiny hope that it will persist for hours, the knowing that it will only exist for a short while and so we stretch it to its limits, holding our attention and praying a phone call, a child, an unimportant question doesn't break the spell.

Cortisol isn't all bad either; it's a steroid hormone produced by the adrenal glands and vital for survival. It's essential for basic bodily functions including the regulation of metabolism, management of the immune and stress response and maintaining blood pressure. But chronic stress can cause dysregulated cortisol secretion, and when cortisol remains high even in the absence of an immediate stress, it can take weeks for this dysregulation to return to normal.

Stress is helpful in short bursts as the ultimate motivator, but it becomes problematic when it's prolonged and we don't have the ability or capacity to cope with it. This is really common for most of us. Statistics show that it's also more prevalent in younger adults – aged 16 to 34 – with housing worries and the pressure to succeed predominant concerns. Millennials are also suffering: almost 50 per cent report symptoms of depression and/or anxiety disorders and 84 per cent report burnout. These concerns are exacerbated by what's largely unavoidable: uncertainty in all facets of life, including social and environmental challenges.

We're only just beginning to understand the effects that stress and uncertainty have on our body, our psyche and our longevity. And yet we also know the remedy: rest. Think of food as fuel and sleep as repair. And in all the small moments of breathing space, there is the opportunity to counteract the effects of modern life with the ancient forms of respite that the body responds to instantaneously.

FIVE WAYS TO ...
Reset your nervous system

1. Relieve your tension by gently shaking your legs, arms and body in a way that feels good. This intuitive movement releases stagnant stress, softens tense muscles and encourages you to breathe more deeply and sigh.

2. Run cold water over your hands for a quick reset for your mind and body that brings your awareness immediately to the present. Cold water on the face and the body also helps activate the parasympathetic nervous system, so try turning the tap to cold at the end of your shower.

3. Hold yourself and breathe with one hand on your heart and the other on your belly, inhaling for a count of four and exhaling for a count of six. This deep breathing disrupts the anxiety circuit in the brain and reminds your nervous system that you're safe.

4. Lie with your legs up a wall, a simple restorative pose that calms the nervous system and reduces stress. Let out a few audible sighs while you're there, and let the bed or the floor hold you; you don't need to hold on here.

5. Step outside (with bare feet, if possible) and become aware of what you can see, hear, feel and smell. This focused awareness on your senses helps to ground you in the moment.

2
An uncluttered brain

Mental clarity is dependent on intentional breathing space and supportive habits – these are what the brain needs to function optimally.

I watch a video of a forest, filmed from directly above the canopy, and I notice that the trees are polite, perhaps even shy, as they make space for each other. The canopy expands and contracts, like an enormous set of lungs, and then I remember that's exactly what they are: lungs of the earth, breathing so we can breathe, too. Every leaf contains pores that act like a mouth, taking in carbon dioxide that's transported to its cells so it can be transformed and released as oxygen.

Perhaps this is why we instinctively breathe more deeply when in green spaces, because we are urged by the trees and leaves to deeply inhale the oxygenated space and feel calmer as a consequence. Nature is clever. You are nature, too. And getting to know yourself is deepening your connection to the world. We may not be able to change the world, but we can change how we inhabit it.

Scientists refer to the brain as a 'neuron forest', because neurons, our nerve cells making up the messaging service that communicates with every part of our body, resemble trees, and they populate the intricate landscape of the brain – all the ridges and valleys – in their billions. The brain is an organ with incredible ability, but it's primarily an instrument of instinct, not logic. It's mostly reactive, not reflective; it makes impulsive decisions in response to threats and temptations, which prompt it to change course immediately. Essentially, the brain is programmed to think that we don't have enough. This *scarcity mindset* means it's natural for us to hoard information and we store it all: memories, recollections, statistics, facts and stories – ghost-like threads. We are inundated with alluring information everywhere we turn, and we are effectively gorging on it, because that's precisely what our brain was designed to do.

The brain is also lazy. It would rather be distracted than interrogated. Creating a calm mind, resilient to this primal behaviour, requires a very conscious pulling back from the brain's impulses so we can consider and reflect, analyse and plan. This is what breathing space is for. In a world that vies for our attention, it's never happenstance; it has to be intentional.

Every day we have upwards of 6000 thoughts, with some resources suggesting that number could reach as high as 60,000. Up to 90 per cent of those thoughts are said to be the same as the day before. This is why changing our thought patterns – making habitual change – is so hard. The brain likes to repeat negative and intrusive thoughts, recycled from days and decades past. These thought loops create ruts in the brain, known paths that we trudge along most days. But as Dr Jack Feldman, professor of neurobiology at the University of California, Los Angeles, has discovered, deep, slow breathing helps disrupt these circuits and get the brain out of well-worn but maladaptive ruts. The brain is not a fixed and static organ; we can exercise it to build new pathways or strengthen weak ones.

These ruts, or neural pathways, are created by habitual behaviour. Habits are automatically triggered behaviours that don't require conscious awareness or deliberate control. They're really important, because they free up mental bandwidth and provide a consistent routine that is comforting for all of us, but especially those who have a neurodivergent brain or are particularly sensitive to uncertainty.

If you want to create space in your mind, you need to think of it much like you think of your body. It requires care in the form of focused periods of intellectual challenge – muscles stretched and strengthened with the fodder of thoughtful stories, rhythmic music, deep breathing and lively conversation – and then quiet to process so it can flourish. The brain loves predictability, but alongside the comfort of routine and habitual behaviour we must accept the inevitability of change. It is, after all, the only constant in life. That and the breath.

Room in your mind

Yutori is a multifaceted Japanese concept that is hard to translate succinctly. Its definition varies: space, elbow room, leeway, allowance, time (to spare). That's why my favourite definition of yutori is room in your mind. It's a sense of mental space, without overwhelming thoughts or worries; it leaves room to think about life and others. Let your intention for today be to savour the world around you, to create room in your mind, to allow spaciousness.

A DEEP BREATH CLEARS THE MIND

After intense periods of stress and feeling overwhelmed, the brain just can't take anything more and it shuts down. It's at these times you might say, *I can't hear myself think*, or there's a sort of emptiness that feels like being both overwhelmed and apathetic. It's hard to care about anything when you can't quite define what you're feeling. It's not a soothing sort of quiet but more an unsettling blankness. This is what happens when we keep pushing through without space to breathe and rest. When we're anxious, our thoughts are so frantic that decision-making, sometimes even speaking coherently, isn't possible either, because we're worried about all the eventualities of what's to come and paralysed by the fear of not knowing. In this panic, the most helpful response is a deep breath.

'Writing and reading about the breath – even just talking about it – is valuable,' says Dr Feldman. This is because controlling our breathing increases our interoception – our awareness of our breathing. This awareness also contributes to a decrease in our stress.

What happens in the brain when we breathe deeply?

Dr Feldman says the answer lies in our brain circuitry: the paths in the brain that can be deeply ingrained but can also be disrupted. He asks me to visualise a circle in motion – this is an anxiety loop as a circuit in our brain, the frantically spinning thought process that doesn't allow for decision-making or coherency.

'To some degree this loop is embedded in a system where there's also a breathing loop in the background,' he says. 'Every couple of seconds you take a breath and that's going to influence the anxiety circuit. If you suddenly take a big, deep breath, that's going to throw that circuit off a little bit.'

Essentially, anxiety loses its momentum when we intentionally breathe deeply, and this is why we feel calmer. It's for this reason that breathing deeply and slowly is a common behavioural treatment for people who have panic disorder. 'It seems to be very effective in overcoming intense panic,' Feldman says. 'It works. We don't know in detail why it works, but I believe it's because it disrupts that circuitry enough for it to take a while for that circuitry to come back or, in the case of a panic attack, it disrupts it enough that the panic has dissipated.'

If thoughts have motion and rhythm – which is more likely if they're habitual – breathing deeply essentially disrupts the motion of stressful, anxious thoughts. Deep breaths send anxious thoughts off-kilter. Breath awareness begets deeper, conscious breathing.

We all breathe without thought, but when we breathe with awareness, our mind and body can change. When we create literal breathing space, we're making space in our body – opening up the dark corners, releasing stagnant energy, allowing thought, blood, breath and energy to flow with ease.

Taking deep breaths is calming because it doesn't activate the neurons that communicate with the brain's arousal centre. Feldman and his team discovered that the part of the brain that controls breathing involves more than 3000 interlinked neurons in the brain stem – dubbed by researchers the 'breathing pacemaker' – that can produce a variety of breath patterns, such as a yawn, a gasp or a sigh.

The effectiveness of sighs

Sighs – the quick addition of a second inhalation before an exhalation, creating an unconscious deep double breath – can have emotional triggers, but they also happen involuntarily every few minutes, regardless of our mood.

Why does it feel so good to sigh? Try it now if you like. You'll notice there is a definitive physical release and your body grows heavy and soft with each intentional exhalation. You will also sigh when you're not aware; it's the body's instinctive stress-release mechanism. Humble, yes, but also very effective.

I was curious about this, particularly when thinking about my children and how a bout of sobbing results in long, calming sighs. I wonder, if the body's response to stress is to sigh, if sighing is a protective mechanism.

When I ask Dr Feldman, he shrugs, smiles. 'We can speculate that yes, it is. All mammals sigh, and they sigh more when they're stressed. Imagine you're a small mammal and you're hiding from a predator. If you're calmer, you're probably less likely to be discovered; you're not moving as much and you're breathing less. If it influences your survival, it's going to stay in the gene pool – survival of the fittest! Over time, the action of breathing – slow breathing or sighing to calm you down – became a reflex that increased the likelihood that you would survive, so it became implicated in the genome. Sighing is a way to calm down. In humans, is it protective? Well, if it calms you down, I'd say in the short and long term it's a good thing.'

This research is relatively new. And yet 6000 years ago in the Hindu culture, breath restraint, or pranayama, was practised because it was known to lower anxiety. We now know that this occurs because brainwave impulses change from beta – active, hard-focused brainwaves associated with muscle contraction and higher anxiety; to alpha – passive, softly focused brainwaves that occur when we're awake but relaxed and restful.

I liken it to moving from a room with bright overhead lights to one with a dim lamp. Everything feels softer and more settled when the breath deepens, the body is grounded and the lights aren't so bright.

Where science meets ancient thought

Science explains what we want to know, but take a deep breath – and then another and another – and you'll experience what can only be called 'breathing space'. We also know that a longer out-breath and an in-breath through the nose stimulates the vagus nerve, which in turn activates the parasympathetic nervous system, moderating cortisol levels. Practise long enough and continual deep breathing results in a shift of consciousness to what we call the meditative state or 'theta' brain waves.

Feldman's work is largely focused on the brain, and he spends most of his time in the lab. He admits, though, that while scientists are sceptics, his curiosity eventually took him out of the lab and into a meditation course.

'I wanted to figure out if everything they were saying about the breath and its calming effects were true,' he says. He leans towards the screen on our Zoom call, tells me he also wanted to know if he could levitate. He hasn't achieved Mr Miyagi status, but he has drunk the kool aid. 'I'm an underpowered, uncontrolled experiment of one, but I have bought into the notion that breathing is not just a distraction; I really believe that the breathing component has an effect on meditation.'

Despite decades of research, he admits that we still have a lot to learn.

'Does this overwhelm you, as a scientist, as a human?' I ask. 'The fact that there's so much we don't know about the brain?'

'There's so much we don't know about so many things.'

Yes, there's that uncertainty again. There's a phrase in Zen Buddhism: 'Not knowing is most intimate.' When we can sit in the state of not knowing – get comfortable there instead of wiggling our way out of it to search for the answer – we experience an intimacy, a connection with the world around us. This is where we get to know ourselves.

All we know is this moment, and that's where the breath is.

Take a micropause
Take a deep breath, ideally through your nose, and let out a sigh. Check in with your body: how are you feeling? Check in with your brain: what are you thinking?

HOW TO BREATHE TO CALM YOUR MIND

'There are hundreds of different styles of breathwork,' Dr Feldman says. 'For most people I say keep it simple, do box breathing. It's the go-to breathing practice for US Navy SEALs. My job is nowhere near as stressful as theirs is, so if it's working for them, it may just work for most people.'

Box breathing, also known as square breathing, requires breathing in and intentionally pausing for a certain number of counts. A typical pattern looks like:

1. *Inhale for a count of four.*
2. *Pause for a count of four.*
3. *Exhale for a count of four.*
4. *Pause for a count of four.*

Feldman says that the most wonderful thing about simple breathing practices is their accessibility. You immediately feel the relaxing benefits. It doesn't cost you anything, there's a low possibility of harm, and it can be done wherever you are. It's a proven method of calming your mind.

Don't get too caught up on the numbers – they exist to hold your awareness on your breath and prevent your thoughts from trailing off elsewhere. There's no point holding your inhalation or forcing your exhalation to reach a certain number.

The actual number of breaths doesn't matter. You're not aiming to achieve 'a perfect breath' here. If you do, that almost defeats the purpose. This is about a gentle and conscious flow of breath that allows you to sink into it, regardless of the number or what it sounds or looks like. And this sinking is the activation of your parasympathetic nervous system, which slows your heart rate and helps you rest and, eventually, sleep.

You can practise at any time of day, but lying in bed at night and breathing deeply, your rib cage like an accordion – gentle expansion and contraction – is also deeply beneficial. The aim here is not to count breaths but simply lengthen the exhalation. Think of your outward breath as the relaxing breath, the letting go.

What are you letting go of? Well, anything really, but often when we consciously breathe, we're letting go of obvious tension. So as you get into the rhythm of your intentional inhalations and exhalations, you may like to soften your body – let it sink into the ground or your bed.

There may be times when it feels too hard because your body resists or your mind wanders. This is really normal. Remember, this isn't about a perfect breath, it's about deepening and lengthening your breath. With practice, you'll get there. I promise, it feels really good, like a bit of mind–body magic.

Rhythmic breathing to feel safe

For some, meaning is found in spiritual teachings and religion, because despite the differences between God and deity, there is a common thread in the intentional focus of attention that becomes habitual through prayer, hymn and mantra. And what these practices do is envelop us in rhythm through repetition. Rhythm is a shared language – between the earth and our most basic selves – and when we ease into it, the world momentarily slows and we do, too.

The practice of breathing in for a count of four and breathing out for a count of six targets the part of our brain involved with the psychological response to panic and stress; our adrenaline levels lower and our attention is restored.

This exact timing is important; it's called the Mayer rhythm of optimal heart–lung function at six breaths per minute. This rhythm is reflected in the Ave Maria Rosary prayer in Latin and Om Mani Padme Om mantra in Sanskrit – both rhythmic formulas that involve breathing at six breaths per minute and thus slow the heart rate.

Allison Davies is a neurologic music therapist who works within a neuro-affirming framework, encouraging and guiding people to better understand their brains through musicality and rhythm. She explains that when we are making sound – praying, singing, chanting out loud or even audibly sighing – it travels from the ears to the brain and is recognised as our unique voice. When you are making sound, your brain interprets it as a safety signal.

'It adds to the data your brain has to tell you what's going on in your environment, which is a helpful way for your brain to determine whether you're safe or not in that moment,' Davies says. 'If we're singing out loud repeatedly, and then the brain recognises our voice and recognises that it sounds calm or confident or loving or compassionate or relaxed, the brain considers that as a safety cue that essentially says: "I'm in a state of control right now."'

And yet for many of us, singing is a challenge because we don't like the sound of our own voice. Davies encourages us to remove our judgement by settling for neutrality in response to the sound of our voice and considering it instead through a neuroscience lens. 'Your brain knows your voice better than any other in the world,' she says. 'Audibly using your voice can help the brain feel safe, especially if we're talking and no one is talking back. It's a sign to the brain that we're in control; we're not being interrupted and we're likely being listened to.'

Why slow breathing works

Slow breathing slows our thoughts by activating the vagus nerve, switching our nervous system into a relaxed state and reducing the activity in the brain centres that are associated with quick-fire, anxious thoughts. Indeed, the first step to creating space in your mind is to slow your breath. A deep breath is your brain's reset button. This ancient practice can take chaotic, distracted thinking to calm and focus within minutes. The more you do it, the stronger your mental resolve. Perhaps most pertinent is the fact that the physiological act of breathing – one you can alter within seconds – gives you control over your brain, the way you're thinking and the emotions you're experiencing.

Space in the mind starts with a deep breath because conscious, slow breaths mitigate stress.

FIVE WAYS TO …
Come back to your breath

1. Remember that your breath is the one constant in life. You can access this inbuilt de-stress tool without anyone else knowing. It calms you in tense situations and brings you to the present moment so you can savour delight.

2. Accept that there's no such thing as a 'perfect' breath and therefore, no need to 'strive' for it. Instead, just let your body and mind follow the flow.

3. Establish a nightly ritual of taking a deep inhalation followed by a pause and then an audible sigh. Do this as many times as it takes for your body to feel softer and heavier. If your mind wanders, mentally repeat 'let' as you inhale and 'go' as you exhale. Focus on breathing into your ribs so they expand and contract like an accordion. The simple process of breath–hold–breath activates your vagus nerve and, consequently, your 'rest and digest' state, which is exactly where you need to be for sleep.

4. Make it your go-to. Whenever you feel tired, distracted, tense or overwhelmed, come back to your breath by counting four breaths in and six breaths out. Write a reminder on a sticky note and put it on your desk or the fridge or the bathroom mirror. It may be a gentle reminder: 'Let go' or a firm directive: 'Breathe!'

5. Let it help you savour the good moments. Mindful deep breathing hones awareness of self and surroundings, so you're more attuned to positive experiences.

3

A safe, nourished body that moves and rests

Your body is a force of nature. Listen to it: it tells you everything you need to know.

Ours is an urgent culture with a time-scarcity mindset: time is money, which means we are billable. But what this fails to recognise or consider is our humanness. We are bones, blood, flesh and breath. We are made of natural matter that evolves, grows, ages, decays and decomposes. We are nature. All things in nature move and live intuitively. We are often the exception.

Despite the fact that in the nineteenth century the *Oxford English Dictionary* defined nature as 'in a wider sense, the whole of the natural world, including humans and the cosmos', a recent edition omitted 'humans'. Thanks to the campaigning of environmental activists Frieda Gormley and Jessie Mond

Wedd, the *OED* has edited the definition back to the original. Now is not the time to actively separate ourselves from nature – in life or in language. We need to be seeking a deeper connection to the natural world to better understand ourselves, because through this ancient practice of connecting with nature we can find breathing space – in trees, sky and ocean, the turning of seasons and shifting of light.

Breathing space is not a lifestyle, it's a basic human need. It's our home base. Creating space in our mind so we can move through the world with a little more awareness – of our body, breath and nervous system – is biologically normal. Being aware of the body is being aware of our needs. But because we live in a world firmly concerned with aesthetics, where even the well-intentioned concept of self-care has been commercialised, the body is considered a temple – precious and revered. And yet we'd probably be more inclined to care for it if we were realistic about the fact that it's simply a house – chipped weatherboard, slightly rusting gutters, life worn into the floorboards, memories incused on the walls. It requires maintenance and upkeep to function well.

After all, the purity and methodical ritual of a temple is a rigidity that feels too cloistered for the human body, a vessel designed for movement, exploration and feeling, for general wear and tear, risk and, sometimes, ruin. All humans are flawed in some way, and yet we strive for perfection. But I think that we perhaps reach the point of contentment when we realise that we're enough, just as we are. New beginnings don't require blank pages. There's no need to reinvent yourself. Instead, you can take small steps to make meaningful change. Sometimes it's most helpful to stay right where you are and take a nap. You almost always feel better after a good sleep.

AN AGEING BODY IS A LIVING BODY

We live in an ageist society that seems to have forgotten a simple truth: if we are ageing, we are living. Growing up is a privilege; growing old is, too. There may be increasing pressure to live and look a certain way, and perhaps not enough emphasis on the confidence and joy that can compound with each year that passes. As we pay attention to what matters and let go of the things that don't, we learn more about who we are. We get to know ourselves. There is an undeniable sense of contentment when we can confidently say, *This is who I am!* and make choices accordingly.

Some of those choices may be in response to your body, which keeps reminding you to slow down and take care. As author Sinéad Gleeson says in her essay collection *Constellations*, 'The body is an afterthought' – until it demands attention in the form of pain. And yet this internal, intuitive messaging system is often quiet at first: a whisper, an ache, a growing sense of unease. You have to turn down the external volume to hear it, and that's because the consistent social messaging is to *keep going*, *be better* and *do better*. Beneath this is the assumption that what we're doing and who we are aren't good enough. We can be intelligent, aware and in tune, and still the tiny wondering exists within us because we live in a late capitalist society and it says, most loudly in periods of doubt, stress and uncertainty: *You should be doing more.* You are not alone in feeling undone.

If we consider how our bodies were designed – and the life they were designed for – we come to realise that we've totally upended the balance. We are still hunters and gatherers, but instead of being people who potter, chat, commune, rest and experience brief periods of threat or high intensity, we are now people who live in an almost constant state of high alert, fuelled and eventually exhausted by spikes in cortisol. This cortisol flood has a primal purpose – it helps us move efficiently to escape danger – but when the perceived danger is persistent, so too are our stress, tension and exhaustion.

Our brains have evolved to survive, but evolution doesn't necessarily have our wellness as a priority. Yes, we can survive. But do we feel well? Are there moments and whole days where you can take a breather and not feel guilty for it? And perhaps most importantly, are you moving through your week with a regulated nervous system or do you constantly feel on edge and flighty, as if a gust of wind or a small inconvenience could dismantle you?

Being realistic about existential exhaustion is helpful. Weariness is a symptom of the modern world, a general sense of malaise that follows us, settles, sometimes sends us off to bed when it's most inconvenient. The truth is we're humans not built for perpetual tasks, yet we exist in a world of chronic cognitive overload. We are effectively inundated with information and it sits within us, compounded by daily tasks and must-dos and the external pressure to get things done and do them well. This is precisely why you can't hear yourself think. It's why sudden noise makes you gasp. It's why you long for some breathing space. It's particularly challenging in times of abject uncertainty and transition, in between phases where you exist on autopilot, comforted by habits and routines because they are stabilising. We lean on what's most dependable when uncertainty abounds.

Sometimes it's in these liminal seasons that we are forced to be most honest about who we are and what we care about. As we move through adulthood we may have more responsibilities – drowning in life admin where the emails, bills, appointments and school permission slips accumulate rapidly – but we often also have more agency. And with this comes choice. And the joy of a life not lived in comparison to others. Negative experiences can't be avoided – life is inherently uncertain and stress is a normal part of our days. But what's required to navigate modern life and its inevitable obstacles is flexibility, and that demands a clear mind and an *energised body*. Our awareness of what we need in the moment is, in part, dependent on our vitality – which stems from rest.

Finding beauty in the cracks

In the Zen Buddhist practice of kintsugi, you take a broken vessel and stick the pieces back together. You don't try to hide the vein-like fractures but instead emphasise them, using gold or silver as the glue. It's a comforting visual for the body, I think. Despite your stress, there are moments in your day when you can rest. A busy schedule hides them; slowing down brings them into view. Breathing space lets the light in.

THE PSYCHOLOGY OF COMFORT

If uncertainty informs stress, the foundation of safety in the body and mind are essential habits that hone our self-awareness. From a sense of security comes calm. We need reliable habits to live well and create reprieve between moments of stress. What feels like safety is going to be different for each of us – because we all start from a different place. While some of us are normally vigilant and reactive, others may be grounded and likely unperturbed by external triggers. But we all connect the feeling of cosiness with safety and stability: it's essentially an emotional cocoon. In fact, when we feel most untethered, we reach for what feels most comforting. It's a form of psychological self-soothing, but from a biological perspective it facilitates the release of oxytocin.

When we are warm and cosy, when we feel safe and secure, oxytocin – aka 'the love hormone' or 'cuddle chemical' – flows and we're filled with the delightful, gooey sense that everything will be okay. The Danish and Norwegian word hygge encompasses this feeling. Aesthetically, it's defined by the hallmarks of nostalgic comfort: candlelight, soft furnishings, warm drinks. At a primal level, oxytocin is the social hormone that ensures our survival and helps us bond with each other, creating an internal version of hygge. In the everyday, it fosters a sense of contentment and wellbeing. It also has healing properties, moderating pain and acting as an anti-stress tonic. It essentially manages the cortisol that charges through our body as we live our life.

Warmth is a salve for our nervous system. It's a really practical way to take care of ourselves because it isn't complicated. Pressing a hot water bottle against your belly, watching comfort television, tucking yourself into bed, slowly sipping tea or coffee or soup, connecting with someone you love, hugging a pet – it's a nurture bath of feel-good energy. And when we're aware of it, we're even more receptive to it. Comfort is care for the body and mind. It's a pocket of space in the busyness of our day. Seek it out, indulge in it. It's the foundation of psychological wellbeing and is a powerful form of rest.

WHAT WE NEED TO FEEL SAFE

When we're exhausted and depleted, we may not even know what we need, so it's easy to spiral into doubt, throw our hands in the air and think: *What's the point?* Let's start by acknowledging our basic needs. Every human is unique, but we all need the same ingredients to survive and foster wellbeing:

- **Water**. *We think more clearly and move with greater ease when we're hydrated.*
- **Food**. *We thrive on a blend of plants, proteins and fats, minimally processed and preferably eaten slowly. Our food is our fuel: it nourishes, supports and strengthens us.*
- **Movement**. *Any kind of movement is good for us, but exercise that increases our heart rate three to four times a week is one of the best ways to care for our brain.*
- **Sleep**. *It's how we repair our body and regulate our emotions. Consider it literal physiological and psychological maintenance.*
- **Sunlight**. *Exposure to the sun directly on our skin boosts our immune system and regulates our sleep cycle by reinforcing our circadian rhythm (our day–night body clock).*

Every time you choose one of these things, remind yourself that you're giving your body energy. Ask yourself one question right now: *What does my body need?* A glass of water, a nap, a brisk walk, a gentle stretch, a week of regular, nourishing meals? Perhaps it needs the confidence to leave things out, because less is more when it comes to the body and a good life.

FIVE WAYS TO ...
Come back to your body

1. Get sun on your face first thing in the morning. Even if it's just for a few minutes, it will reinforce your circadian rhythm and help relieve the heaviness of unsettled sleep.

2. Move your limbs. Shake your arms and legs while you're waiting for the kettle to boil, reach to the sky to release upper back tension and breathe deeply while you stretch.

3. Hold a hot water bottle to your belly. There's nothing more soothing than a heavy heat pressed against your core. It's a prescription for anyone who feels untethered or achy, agitated or overwhelmed.

4. Go to nature. Lie on the grass, sit under a tree, pull some weeds, plant some seedlings. The best way to ground yourself is to be on the ground, hands immersed in the soil, mind distracted by the minutiae, breath deepening.

5. Swap a scroll for a stroll. Put your phone down and go for a wander instead. It loosens your muscles and your mind.

4
Breathing space

*'Free time' is no longer common vocabulary,
but this ancient habit is a simple remedy to
feeling overwhelmed and exhausted.*

If modern life has eradicated breathing space, we need to
reinstate it for ourselves. It answers so many of our deep-seated
questions about how we can stay well in a world that is
increasingly uncertain and, at times, pushing us to the edge.
If we don't create space for ourselves, our body and brain will
force us to. We can be smart here and acknowledge it for what
it is: rather enjoyable prehab now instead of lengthy rehab
when we're at our most vulnerable.

How do you define a shapeless form that doesn't look a
certain way or fit neatly into a timeframe? Breathing space is
nothing and many things: it is what you need it to be in the

moment, and so in this regard it's fluid – a nap, a walk, a rest, a breath.

Creating space isn't about escaping life. It's more about uncovering the gaps between grocery shopping, loading the washing machine and calling the insurance company to request a bill extension. A life with space isn't necessarily easier or without work, but it is more sustainable.

Let's be honest, the world worships work. With wall-to-wall wi-fi and praise for productivity, switching off is getting harder. We are obsessed with efficiency and optimisation, yet if we look at the science, the facts are clear – in order to be creative, productive and well, we require breathing space. Space in the mind is a basic human need. The fact that we don't talk about 'free time' any more is problematic. Across nine books, British psychoanalyst Marion Milner continually referred to 'free time' and creativity as vital parts of a fulfilling life. In her second book, *An Experiment in Leisure,* published in 1937, she commented on the 'growing uneasiness over the anti-intellectual trends of modern life'. Today that's our normal: tech has trumped the imagination, free time is considered a waste, and we're fighting for creative minds to be valued in our society. It feels like free or spare time just doesn't exist in our lexicon, but if we don't speak of breathing space, how can we value it? Look at hobbies – once a way to relax and create, enjoying the process, they're now labelled as a 'side hustle'. Everything is framed in terms of earning potential. We've leached the sacred from the simple, enjoyable things in life that allow us to exist in the moment and experience incidental mindfulness – relieving stress and simultaneously bolstering our mental wellbeing.

HOW TO PRIORITISE BREATHING SPACE

The key to prioritising breathing space is to find value and meaning in it. The first step is acknowledging that its value is evidence-based and scientifically proven. Our need for breathing space is a fact based on our evolutionary biology. When we begin to pay attention and shift our habits accordingly, we're responding to what we innately need. This is a necessary step as we begin to live more intentionally and simultaneously get to know ourselves. Breathing space gives us room to grow.

Feeling overwhelmed is a symptom of overload – too much data, noise, information and obligation. When we understand the brain, and in particular its instinctive responses, we come to realise that it's not bad habits that see us indulge in everything that's on offer, it's human nature. This knowledge helps relieve the guilt we may feel when we wonder: *Why am I like this?* But guilt can also be helpful. It can prompt us to shift our priorities and create new habits.

I think we can start valuing breathing space by acknowledging that it *is* productive. It's not a waste. You're not frittering away precious hours. Rather, you're giving your brain the opportunity to switch from constant hard focus to interspersed periods of soft fascination. When our brain metaphorically takes a breather, clears out the clutter and has the free time to explore potential, imagine, create, dream, we experience soft fascination. Our body does the same after an intense workout: our muscles are switched on during our run and when we get home they soften and relax. And then, when we give them time to recover, they will perform well the next time we head out to exercise. Our brain is similar. When we have breathing space, we're sequestering energy, so that we can be productive when we need to be, with less procrastination and greater clarity.

Yes, it's all well and good to promote a slow life, but you still have to get things done. This is where we get tripped up, throw our hands up in the air and think: *What's the point?*

There's an undeniable buzz when we get to tick an item off our to-do list and for the rest of the day think: *Yes! I got that done.* Doing is innately satisfying, but I wonder if it's possible to just *do* nothing? By definition, *nothing* is no thing, not anything. *Nothingness* is worthlessness or insignificance. No wonder we find it so hard to value it. There's also no tangible measure of breathing space. In fact, it looks different for all of us, which is complicated because we generally like to measure our effort against each other, to prove that it's worthwhile, to motivate us to continue. Define 'nothingness' for yourself.

You can start right now, if you like.

Breathing space is not segregated to weekends or holidays or to the scraps of days that you look forward to when everything else is done. Breathing space is little moments of time, often. It's a few breaths here, 10 minutes there, sometimes an hour between one thing and another.

You could perhaps start with 10 minutes of nothing once a day, and observe how it makes you feel. 'Nothing' could be lying like a starfish on your bed or sitting under a tree and staring off into the distance. It could be getting cosy in your favourite chair and surrounding yourself with pillows while you hug a hot water bottle. All of these things look like nothing, but what they actually are is *active rest*. Sometimes we value something if it has a name and a purpose; we're more inclined to prioritise it if we know it's worthwhile. For many of us, scientific evidence solidifies this.

Redefining self-care

Self-care may have valuable roots in Black feminist activism but, like many things, it's been hijacked by late capitalist culture. We're encouraged to buy more stuff so we feel more whole, but the opposite is also true: the 'stuff' adds to our responsibilities and obligations and we end up feeling stuck and stagnant. Ten-step skincare routines are glorified, but they don't relieve the mental load; if anything they add to it. We seem to have forgotten that the time we spend working to buy our 'self-care' of choice could be time used to rest and retreat. We've got things the wrong way round.

Sometimes it can be helpful to stop and ask yourself: what actually matters to me? What do I believe in? What is my moral code? I write these questions and stop to notice a small bird flit from branch to branch in the hedge that hugs my front garden. The bird gathers supplies in its beak – leaves, dried grass, twigs as fine as splinters, wisps of dog hair – to build its spring nest. I watch it over days, this female wren, small enough to fit in my hand, light enough to be carried by the winds that sweep over the island at this time of year. Noticing these small, precious things matters to me. I want to always have space in my day to sit and pay attention to a bird in a tree, a tiny gatherer reusing what was once something else.

Is this all I need to know about myself to make change? Perhaps. What I'm certain of is that it's a marker. If I don't feel like I have the time to sit and observe what's happening outside my window, my day is too full. Because this breathing space – a small gap in my day – offers mental reprieve and, more importantly, a profound sense of hope. It's deeply satisfying to know this. A recent study on mental wellbeing found that we feel better in spaces with environmental biodiversity because we can see birds and hear birdsong.

The meat of life

Research shows that happiness isn't found in goal attainment but in the process of working towards goals. Jamaican novelist and screenwriter Sara Collins may have been referencing her process to create compelling fictional characters, but she believes we 'Live life in the gap between yearning and getting. That's where the meat of life is.'

And this meat, this goodness, is centred in everyday tasks: the first thing we do when we wake in the morning, the pace at which we move through the world, the food we prepare and eat, the small interactions we have as our day goes on, the words we share with the barista, our friendly nod to the elderly man watering his garden, the things we notice, the things we don't, the necessary space between a spark of an idea and the completion of a project.

This space – this yearning – is increasingly rare because we live in a culture of immediate gratification. Yet step into a garden, spend time with an artist, chat to a research scientist or simply observe a pregnant woman, and you'll see that time exists but cannot be rushed or sped along. Life – nature – happens in the waiting, the space between yearning and getting.

BURNOUT

We need breathing space so we don't burn out. For anyone with burnout, hope feels very far away.

You can make a home within your own skin, where you are contained under one roof, aware of your footings, the elements that made you who you are today. But when you start to feel unstable, when the roof starts leaking and the paint cracks and the weeds overgrow, insidious and almost joyfully stubborn, a general sense of weariness descends and you may start to feel defeated. You may even feel homesick at the discomfort of the unfamiliar, a longing to return to what you know, even though you're right where you've always been.

This sense of being overwhelmed coupled with exhaustion and perhaps apathy – even if it's not fully formed – is becoming more common. These are the three main official symptoms of burnout, and while that word has been popularised in recent years and perhaps diluted as a consequence, it's also recognised as a global epidemic. If home is your reference point in the world, it's understandable that you'll feel lost – a sense of being all at sea – when it feels like it's falling apart.

If you feel a little worn out, perhaps deep, conscious breaths are just the invigorating habit you need to embrace. When you're carrying a bone-deep weariness, though, any suggestions for improvement can feel too hard. Sometimes the best thing you can do is curl up in bed and wait till you feel better.

Burnout is not the kind of fatigue that can be healed with a good night's sleep. Rather, it's an exhaustion rooted in your bones, the kind that makes your limbs heavy and your brain slow. The simplest of everyday tasks – making breakfast, responding to an email, washing your hair – can feel impossible.

Healing from burnout – or even back-pedalling while you're burning out – requires surrender, an intentional retreat from the outside world. It demands you listen to your body, slow down and honour your needs. Recovering from any illness or a period of deep grief after loss requires the acceptance that you're in a new season where rest comes before anything else. Life must pivot and it can, if you let it. This is a process – often a slow one – where you unravel the ties that bind you to a life of doing, so that you can eventually find purpose and meaning in rest. Often this is a liminal period in life where you make change, and it can be deeply challenging.

Burnout has been popularised in recent years, but as Gordon Parker, Scientia professor of psychiatry at UNSW and founder of the Black Dog Institute, explains, it's not a modern affliction. 'It dates back to the fifth century AD, when it was known as "acedia" – an inability to work or pray.' Dutiful monks, considered the most faithful and attentive to prayers and spiritual work, would wake one day questioning the meaning of life – or whether there was meaning at all.

Returning to earth

How do you come back to yourself? Well, you can start by planting your feet. Spread your toes and press down into the earth – barefoot, regardless of the weather – because this simple connection, of skin to earth or grass or sand, gets you out of your head and into your body. You may think, *What's the point of taking off my socks?* But trust me, it's quick and it works. Shaking your arms helps too, as does stretching your body intuitively for five minutes, slowly releasing all the pent-up energy and loosening the knots. Shift your weight from one foot to the other until you find a comfortable point of balance. Here you'll begin to feel some semblance of stillness.

What is burnout?

People everywhere are experiencing some level of burnout. They may not be curled up in bed unable to get up, but they're getting to the end of each day dragging themselves through routines, with eyes that sting and a brain that can't find the words. Perhaps you exist on the adrenaline that you're sure you can feel pumping through your body. Maybe you cry at the littlest of inconveniences or you've lost the confidence and motivation you once had. Instead of a problem-solving brain that always finds the right words at the right time, you now wonder if you've got a brain at all, so foggy, forgetful and slow it is. 'It's a lot,' we mutter to ourselves and our friends, a defeated consolation. Sometimes we feel like we can't cope any longer, but because we're too exhausted to make even one more decision, we distract ourselves by scrolling, which drains our attention even more, and so the cycle goes.

Burnout isn't currently recognised in the *Diagnostic and Statistical Manual of Mental Disorders* (*DSM*), despite the fact that in 2019 the World Health Organization (WHO) classified it as a syndrome, defined as 'an occupational phenomenon resulting from chronic workplace stress that has not been successfully managed'. Professor Parker is conflicted by this, saying there are valid arguments for and against burnout being listed as a syndrome. 'If it's not a psychiatric condition, people are going to be comfortable talking about it. They're comfortable saying they're burning out or they're burnt out because there's no stigma attached to it. If we were to make it a psychiatric condition, that has some impact. On the other hand, what's good for the goose is good for the gander: if *DSM* has acute and chronic stress reactions, and burnout is, in a sense, a stress reaction, then why wouldn't it be included?'

Parker and his team have broadened the original definition of burnout to include:

- *exhaustion*
- *cognitive impairment*
- *lack of 'feeling tone' – people just don't get a buzz out of anything, there's no joie de vivre*
- *withdrawal insularity – instead of going to have lunch with colleagues, you may go and sit in the canteen by yourself*
- *compromised work performance*
- *associated symptoms of anxiety, insomnia and compromised immune function.*

It can be helpful to remember that, as humans, we innately seek meaning. But sometimes, or perhaps a lot of the time, meaning is hard to come by. When we exist in these moments – which may stretch over days or weeks – we feel disenchanted and lacklustre. Motivation is low and productivity is, too. This permeating sense of apathy, which washes everything dull and halts any creative thinking, is one of the symptoms of burnout.

Yet today, for millennials and generation Zers, burnout can also be existential: *What is my purpose? What do I believe in? Where should I go next?* And these questions often come all at once, when a great emotional unravelling occurs with the weight of big decisions. When work is demanding (and perhaps uncertain), it's difficult to step away and choose to rest. You are at the whim of your brain, which is inevitably thrown by exhaustion, an influx of information, distractions and stress. There are always warning signs – gentle nudges from your body and brain to step back and slow down – but it's difficult to heed that advice when you find yourself working longer and more arduously. We are a generation of chasers, feeling like we can never quite make the mark and simultaneously can't afford to take a breather. And then we are stopped by life, weathered by the routines and obligations that shape us.

Technology was supposed to make life easier, but we're working harder than ever. Perhaps most pertinent is the fact that our identity is so closely connected with our profession. The work we do – how much we get done and the quality of it – is a direct reflection of our self-worth. And while four-day working weeks have been trialled and both employers and economists nod to the fact that productivity doesn't decline when we spend fewer hours in the office, busyness is a modern measure of social status, according to sociologist Jonathan Gurshuny. Our culture celebrates workaholism.

For creatives, who are encouraged to churn out content instead of making art, burnout is much the same: anxiety, feeling overwhelmed and exhausted, inhibiting any sort of creative flow, despite how often we bring ourselves to the page or the easel. Procrastination and distraction are likely to send us scrolling, and so we end up in a comparison trap that feeds our self-doubt and further inhibits our creativity. This is the loop many of us exist in, and sometimes big emotional shake-ups in the form of mental illness, relationship breakdowns or career pivots force us to question our life's purpose and our choices. They also force us to get to know ourselves: what we need to live well, what we can and can't tolerate, how much we *feel*, and how we can tune in and listen to our body so we nourish it adequately.

Are you on your way to burnout?

You may know this exhaustion, the sudden realisation that you couldn't possibly make one more decision. It's like your brain has abruptly decided to switch off: you feel disconnected and ineffective. Except this spiral is not sudden at all. It's the end result of a progressive slowing down as your brain struggled to keep up with demand – to plan, foresee, schedule, reassess, make decisions and solve problems. All of these things get increasingly difficult as we slip further into burnout. This exhaustion prompts a sense of not caring because caring requires energy, and few of us have any to spare. When we don't care, we start to question the worth in everything we do, and along the way we lose sight of what matters and what gives life meaning.

Our brains are perfectly designed to be engaged and focused on the present moment: calm and alert – a daily reality for our ancestors 10,000 years ago. They're not designed for the persistent mode we force them into today: the constant looking ahead while we continuously process information and juggle demanding work and life schedules. This often involves the need to make decisions, reassess plans, solve problems and create content while we fight and succumb to the persistent distraction from phones and the expectation to keep up with social media notifications, WhatsApp messages and emails. This is particularly apt for people with higher acute sensory processing sensitivity, who tend to have stronger reactions to stimuli, increased emotional sensitivity and a rich inner life (it's not a weakness but does require a more intentional and ultimately slower pace of living).

How to create space in your mind and care for your brain? Do something every day that your ancestors would have done 10,000 years ago: nap under a tree; go outside at night and stargaze; wake with the sun; gather with friends, share a meal and tell a story; pay attention to the trees; make something with your hands; light a fire; draw something that's meaningful to you.

Mental exhaustion has different levels, but we all know the fog or the frazzle of feeling overwhelmed and overworked. It's only exacerbated by the supposed solution: fitting more 'self-care' into our day. *My brain hurts*, you may say. And yet you keep going – pushing through – to tick those items off your to-do list and meet that deadline, consoling yourself with the fact that you're being productive. You're being a 'good' human.

How to avoid burnout

Your mind is not a machine. If you find yourself saying, 'I'll rest later,' consider this a clue that you're on a collision course and you're most likely burning out. If you're in this state – or you're familiar with it – you know that it's really hard to see a way out, mostly because a way out requires you to make another decision. If you find yourself thinking, *I don't have time for that right now*, this is what you need to do:

1. **Drink a glass of water**, *slowly.*
2. **Look out into the world**. *Let your eyes focus and rest softly on the sky, or the leaves of a tree, a bird on a rooftop, drops of rain falling down the window.*
3. **Inhale and then sigh**. *Do this three times, or as many times as you need to feel some sense of space in your body.*

You don't need to make a big decision today. Instead make a small one: choose to go to bed early.

Parental and autistic burnout

New research suggests that burnout isn't solely dictated by profession or connected to the workplace. Parental burnout is now considered a clinical phenomenon and has been reported across global communities. Autistic burnout is also expected for those who receive a diagnosis later in life and is often the catalyst for seeking a diagnosis. For many autistic people, it is also recurring and impacts functioning, mental health, quality of life and wellbeing. Allison Davies, a neurologic music therapist who works with neurodivergent people, reiterates that a life spent trying to fit in is a life where you don't belong. 'This is a normal experience for autistic people. Because we live in systems that don't meet our needs, we're constantly trying to keep up with the pace of others and adhering to neuronormativity. The burnout comes from that – whether it's before or after a diagnosis.'

Questioning whether you're neurotypical can happen at any time, but there are often triggers – and for new parents, postpartum is one of them. The sudden loss of routine coupled with sensory overload can push them outside their window of tolerance. When reliable structures no longer exist, self-managing or masking becomes increasingly difficult, and the burden on the body is significant, resulting in profound fatigue and sometimes co-occurring health conditions.

One study of 42 countries shows that the highest prevalence rates of parental burnout are in Western countries, where there are high expectations of parents yet low levels of social support. For mothers in particular, the work is round the clock and relentless; the maternal brain may be more resilient to stress and boredom, but parenting was never designed to be a solo effort. In heterosexual relationships, the mother is typically responsible for the primary care load throughout the day, evening, night and into what's known as the woman's 'fourth shift': overnight and into the next morning. For most of our evolutionary history, we have lived in small groups where alloparenting was the norm. Newborn babies as young as three weeks old were cared for by adults other than the parents for up to 40 per cent of the time. This is the 'village' we're currently missing, and it's contributing to burnout and increasing rates of loneliness and mental illness.

A break away from family life – reprieve in the form of 24 hours alone in a hotel room – is a dream, and some new mothers feel so desperate for an enforced rest that they consider a minor car accident or a broken limb to justify an unexpected but relatively peaceful hospital stay. It even has a name: 'the hospital fantasy'. I know this deep exhaustion coupled with almighty responsibility and obligation well. And now, a little further into my parenting journey, I know that the only way to create breathing space in those intense and physically arduous early years – where you're always juggling, one way or another – is to make it a priority, to carve it out in the middle of things, to find some space among the chaos. It means turning away from the work – which is never actually 'done' – and choosing instead to move or breathe or rest.

'Yes,' you may think, 'that's exactly what I need to do,' but doing it may be a little harder, because the symptoms of parental burnout make executive functioning – firm and intentional decision-making followed by actionable steps – quite difficult. And it's about this time that many mothers will look at the mess of the family home, think they should be reading to their child or taking them to the park, feel guilty that they can't do any of these things and perhaps begin to question their worth (this is the insidious and harmful nature of shame when we compare our everyday reality with the idealised images of motherhood). In my extensive research as a health journalist, perinatal health specialists collectively agree that it's never been harder to be a mother; the increasing mental health issues aren't so much psychological conditions but a normal human response to a highly stressful situation.

There are many big influences at play here, including a lack of reverence and respect for new parents, as evidenced in the perpetuation of the 'perfect mother' myth, and a significant lack of social support.

Resulting from chronic parental stress, the four main symptoms of parental burnout are:

1. *physical and/or emotional exhaustion*
2. *questioning the quality of our parenting, or feeling shame that we're not good enough*
3. *feeling overwhelmed with responsibility and the relentlessness of it*
4. *difficulty bonding with our baby.*

A capitalist society – particularly one focused on progress and productivity – benefits immensely from good people striving to do good things. The drive to work, to achieve and perfect, to tick the boxes and take care of everyone and everything is deeply rooted in women in particular. Unpicking this hardwired belief is a practical way to prioritise the breathing space you know you need. This space is beneficial for children, too. There's a correlation between less time 'being' in nature – playing freely, roaming, exploring – and declining mental health for children and teenagers.

REST REQUIRES SELF-COMPASSION

Workplace, creative and parental burnout require the same remedy: rest. But first this requires self-compassion. In her 2019 survey 'The Rest Test', psychologist and BBC radio presenter Claudia Hammond found that for many people rest was associated with anxiety and guilt. You probably know that niggling sense of *I should be doing this* that prevents you from taking time out. When there's so much to do and so few opportunities to do it, how can we prioritise moments and hours of conscious rest? What helps is a very clear understanding of how our brain works and what it requires to function well. With this understanding comes a solid connection: rest eventually equates to clear thinking and problem-solving – in other words, productivity.

The truth is, we're not very good at taking care of ourselves, at prioritising what's physiologically and psychologically beneficial. And perhaps that's because when time is pressing and obligations are rife, the easiest thing to drop is what seems most superfluous. Therein lies our collective dilemma – valuing the small moments of care enough to cherish them takes considered effort (and the will to protect them when life gets in the way). But here's the thing, you don't have to have all the answers to know that you need care. And it may seem totally self-indulgent at a time when the world's problems are gnawing at us regardless of our perceived distance from them. Is it even morally appropriate for us, in our near perpetual comfort, to create even more space for ourselves?

I think it is, because it fortifies us against adversity and burnout. It's what we need to navigate normal, everyday life and to advocate for social and political change.

FIVE WAYS TO …
Navigate feeling overwhelmed as a parent

1. Admit that you're overwhelmed. Say it out loud: 'This is really hard, I feel really stressed' (this fosters self-awareness) and then remind yourself that a hard day doesn't necessarily mean it will be a hard week. It's also helpful to acknowledge that parenting today is innately challenging. Feeling overwhelmed is not a reflection of your ability or effort. You're not flawed, you're a human, likely caring for a baby with minimal support. We were never meant to parent this way.

2. Cultivate a mindset of surrender. There's a lot you can't control in parenthood, but you can practise self-compassion, which looks like lowering your ideals, embracing a 'good-enough' mindset and surrendering to the unpredictable flow of life with small children. Parenthood requires almost constant pivoting, especially when it comes to plans and goals. Your worth as a parent is not judged on the tidiness of your home, your body size or shape, the way you birthed, or your choice to stay home or return to paid work.

3. Go outside and ground yourself. Studies show that when new parents leave the house (particularly the stressors of mess and unfinished jobs) and spend time in nature, they experience improved mental health, in part because they feel joy in watching their baby experience the world. This sensory stimulation also improves infant sleep.

4. Seek out incidental conversations. Everyday conversation with your barista, the person at the bus stop and other parents is an early mental health intervention. Fostering a sense of connection also prompts the release of oxytocin, which moderates stress.

5. Lean on safety habits when you're stressed. Firstly, remind yourself that you're not being chased by a predator, and then do what's most practical in the moment: drink a glass of water slowly, stretch your arms up to the sky, take three deep breaths followed by three audible sighs, run cold water over your hands.

PART TWO

How to Create

Your New Normal

This isn't about creating an immaculate life but a sustainable one, where slowness yields more than speed. If we look to the natural world we see that it's loose around the edges. It sprawls and meanders when rain and warmth are abundant, and when drought or frost hit it slows and retreats to preserve its energy, to protect the parts of itself that are more sensitive to the extremes. There is beauty in this surrender, which at first glance looks both minimal and hardy but is actually a wizened sort of resilience. Even when a plant grows or a flower blossoms, it has periodic moments of contraction before shooting upwards and outwards. I like that analogy for life: temporary retreat is vital for productive growth.

Psychologist Dr Elissa Epel has spent most of her career examining the effects of stress on the body. She emphasises that stress is unavoidable, but she also believes we're in control of how we respond to it. And we can counterbalance it with two things:

1. *getting comfortable with uncertainty*
2. *deep rest.*

'If we can practise becoming more comfortable with uncertainty, reminding ourselves with mindfulness that we don't know the future, the next moment, the next year, we can get more used to embracing the present without clutching at it or trying to control it. The awareness of this paradox we live in – only the present moment – helps us live with ease,' she says.

She believes that for those of us living in cities – close to 70 per cent of the world's population – our lifestyle isn't conducive to a sustainable, well life: 'it's too fast-paced, with too many demands – and for too many of us!' Research shows that the part of the brain that senses danger becomes overactive in city-dwellers when they are under stress, leading to a higher incidence of anxiety and mood disorders. Leaving the city may be a short-term solution for some, but it's also not possible or preferable for most people. So what's the next step?

Green social prescribing – supporting people to engage with nature and nature-based activities – has been shown to be an effective way of bolstering physical and mental health. Avik Basu, an environmental psychologist at the University of Michigan's School for Environment and Sustainability, believes that integrating green spaces into urban environments is essential for wellbeing. It's a theory that has gained significant traction, and studies support the protective effects of exposure to nature, especially for mental health and cognitive function. You don't need to live near a forest to benefit. Experiencing small parcels of nature – seeing trees, hearing birdsong, tending to a plant (an active form of care) – relieves psychological stress and attention fatigue. Immersing ourselves in nature is not just an ancient habit, it's the only way we evolved to live. It's our inherent normal; a screen-based sedentary existence is not.

Nature is our natural habitat, and yet modern life is focused on the evaporation of time and also opportunity. That's why we always feel like we're chasing – because we feel like we might miss out. When we create a new normal, we immediately place ourselves in the 'other' camp. When we're othered, we're on the outer. Yes, it can be lonely here, but many of us are questioning modern life and what's considered normal, letting go of the desire to have it all and choosing to settle into a softer existence. This isn't a neat quick fix with standard instructions. It's more of a slow noticing that requires listening and waiting, becoming aware of the things that aren't necessarily valued or seen as worthy in a busy world. The point is that there's no one way of creating breathing space, but knowing how to start is helpful.

A life with pockets of breathing space is softer and sustainable – more easeful. And it's this ease – what some refer to as mindfulness – that has been proven to benefit creativity and productivity. In a world focused on time savoured and time lost, we skirt around the concept of space, perhaps because it's so elusive. Of course, it expands and contracts just as life ebbs and flows, and while you can intentionally create it, it fills quickly, too.

Elaborate, deliberate self-care is not the answer; getting to know your brain and tuning in to your body is. It's no-plan, low-effort, feel-good-in-the-moment actions that are, in their most basic no-frills form, care. This isn't about discipline, it's about awareness: of yourself and the season you're in. It's really getting back to your innate biology and starting with the foundational essentials – sunlight, movement, rest. It's slowing down to check in with yourself: *What do I need in this moment?* And from there you'll learn to reach for the habits that support, settle and ground you – as outlined in the chapters that follow – regardless of where you are and how you live.

FIVE WAYS TO …
Create space in the moment

These are questions you can ask yourself when you feel overwhelmed. They may help you let go of competing thoughts and obligations, to create more space in the moment.

1. Can I say no to this or reschedule? Our priorities tend to get muddled when we're overwhelmed by life and work. Remember, 'No' is a complete sentence.

2. Have I taken care of myself today? This looks like a glass of water, a few deep breaths, stepping outside for five minutes, eating a nourishing meal, going to bed early.

3. What is most important at this moment? Write a list of everything you need to do and put a star next to your priorities. By creating a sense of order, you're relieving that overwhelmed feeling.

4. Am I comparing myself to people I don't know on socials? Slow down for a moment, step to the side and then carry on at your own pace. It's a really lovely way to live.

5. What matters to me in the big scheme of things? Your answer will remind you where you should be directing your time and energy.

1
Pay attention to the gaps

When we're aware of our need and intention to slow down, that's the biggest first step. In a distracted world, awareness is a feat. Asking yourself what you need is learning to pay attention; this is how you care for yourself.

Ordinary life may require increasingly more from us, but we can choose to reinstate the breathing space that's been pushed to the side. The nature of our stress is its persistence: there is no clear beginning or end of the crisis we find ourselves in. And while the stressors may be considered small – an urgent work email, a deadline, overlapping commitments – our brain considers them a potential threat to our existence. It would be funny if it weren't so true.

How to rein the space back in? It's not necessarily a quick fix, but what breathing space mostly requires is our attention, the precious resource that modern life squanders.

Attention, says David Foster Wallace in his essay *This Is Water*, gives us a resounding sense of freedom in a stressful existence. 'But of course there are all different kinds of freedom, and the kind that is most precious you will not hear much talk about in the great outside world of winning and achieving and displaying. The really important kind of freedom involves attention, and awareness, and discipline, and effort.'

How can we create space?

- *Pay attention to the gaps.*
- *Foster awareness of the space that exists.*
- *Stay disciplined so it's protected.*

In an attention economy, this is consistent work. But anything that you practise often and with intention fast becomes a habit. I think it's helpful to consider it as *life work*, not the jobs that pay the bills, but the ones that contribute to your contentment, that bolster your resolve and provide enough reprieve so you can move back into the world feeling a little more like yourself.

In a society where self-care has been commercialised and therapy-speak is everyday vernacular, where our primary purpose is achievement and we strive to be 'useful', we've lost ourselves along the way. Sometimes you may feel like you need to be 'more' or 'less' instead of being just who you are. Mostly, we just need reassurance that wherever we are in life, we're okay.

This is a choice you can make right now, if you like.

LEAVING THE GROWTH MINDSET BEHIND

As we progress through adulthood, our desire to obtain bigger and better, to improve and impress, becomes socially ingrained. This progression is the default life, marked by established social expectations in a series of steps: education, career, marriage, children, property, promotion – and a holiday to escape from the life that requires increasingly more from us. And while many of us find ourselves questioning this existence and contemplating a different way, there's often a big gap between intentions and reality. You may want to make change, but what are the steps involved and are they even possible? For the perennially stressed, it's hard to contemplate, let alone create, a new reality.

No matter our age, busyness is connected to status and worth. But burning out isn't a badge of success either. As we age and become a little wiser, we tend to figure out what really matters in the midst of it all. And perhaps that's where we've found ourselves, in a world of limitless opportunities and increasing challenges. What we most want is permission to live with lower expectations and at a slightly slower pace, dictated more by instincts than schedules.

You can give yourself that permission. Please don't wait for someone else to present it to you. If you do, it may never come.

When we have space for reflection that allows us to enter a contemplative state, we can often formulate our own best advice for how to live well. Getting there isn't always easy though; our intuition is often drowned out by busy schedules, an overwhelming to-do list, family responsibilities, fear and doubt. Modern life isn't conducive to quiet moments for mulling, questioning and reflecting, because modern life has essentially eradicated breathing space.

This simple question: *What do I need?* doesn't always have a straightforward answer, either. But asking it is a practical step, because in doing so, you're starting to pay attention. Prioritising it is tricky, because the internalised marker of a 'good day' is a productive one: got a lot done, ticks on the to-do list, benches cleared, inbox zero, deadlines met, people pleased.

Truth is, you can have the satisfaction of crossing another to-do off the list, but there will always be something else to replace it. Ambition isn't a dirty word, but joy isn't a social priority either, and what this leads to is an imbalance in our drive to be productive and our innate need to rest, seek reprieve and, essentially, be content in doing nothing. If we look to nature, everything is growing, but not overtly and not at an unsustainable pace. Adopting a slow-growth mindset is helpful here: be like lichen or sequoia tress – both grow 1–2 millimetres a year and they thrive when they are undisturbed – when they have space and time.

Breathing space is where we come back to ourselves

When we consider breathing space, and the things preventing us from accessing it, we need to be honest about smartphones and the fact that many of us are caught in a vortex of overuse.

Outrage at technology is nothing new: medieval monks were appalled at the development of 'the book'. But with access to all the information – and the world – there is a sense of sameness, that we are all trundling along a similar fast-paced path, following fleeting trends. As Henry James wrote in *The Wings of the Dove*: 'You're familiar with everything, but conscious, really, of nothing.' And with this sacrifice we've unknowingly made, we've also given away our attention. In an attention economy, what we crave is what James described as 'an empty cup of attention' – a well of quiet, an intentional tending to ourselves in the form of momentary stillness.

When we don't have intentional downtime in the form of breathing space, we lose sight of ourselves. We stop caring, because we don't have the energy. We're so busy that we stop attending to life – to each other and ourselves within it. This is exacerbated when we're in midlife and sandwiched between (still) needy older children and ageing parents; or in early parenthood or at the peak of our career. At these times of life, the space and time to sit back and observe can feel like an impossibility. There is always something to do, and if you don't do it now you'll just have to do it later. On the flipside, there's also the opportunity to do nothing, which requires you to say no, to bow out, to step to the side while the rush of people continues on ahead of you, running a race they're not always aware of.

Breathing space is a practice; it's not something you can outsource or buy. There's no quick fix or a promised outcome. There's no way you can skip the process either; muddling through and figuring things out is how you change a life. If you want to create more space, you need to accept that it will be slow at first.

START SMALL

A single, deep breath. And then another as you look up and out and let your attention land softly on the sky, which, no matter where you are and how you live, amplifies your smallness and helps you put your problems into perspective. This is often when you'll be drawn back to the information portal in the palm of your hand that is constantly encouraging the perfection of a curated life. We are trapped in a feedback loop of external validation, and it takes some really conscious work to pull back from that and find contentment in the ordinariness of our own lives.

A quiet life with space to breathe is less performative and more personal. It's about letting go a little and accepting the messy parts, the ugly bits not for show – the truest things.

Space exists when you stop grasping and leaning forward into life. It exists when you come to realise that you can't control what unfolds beyond your door but you can rest easy in the simple habits you create for yourself. In a world that pushes our productivity, this isn't necessarily convenient, but it does make us more settled, efficient and creative humans. It edges us back to our true selves. This is about protecting a part of yourself that doesn't need to be shared with the world: the space in your mind required for a gentle life.

This ancient habit is an ongoing practice that requires awareness, a gentle pulling back when you get swept up in 'doing' mode. Flow exists when rest does, too. I know that when I enter the productivity vortex – when I feel like I can't take a break because *There's so much to do!* – this is when I need space most.

And yet pulling back from a life of optimisation to stop – the rarity of it, the relief! – isn't so simple. And it's definitely not easy. Being still and quiet is, at first, uncomfortable. It's normal to panic, to fear falling into a rut and getting stuck there. It's normal to fear that you've forgotten something and for a sense of unease to arise. And then you're distracted by those thoughts, trying to figure out what you should be doing rather than sitting and attending to the space in front of you.

Wide, open space is equally alluring and frightening, mostly because it amplifies our smallness. We have a paradoxical (and likely primal) fear of open space because we're not protected there; the uncertainty of life is more pronounced.

We can long for breathing space and, when we finally find it, not know what to do with ourselves. This sense of not knowing can make us panic, but it's also where we learn. In the emptiness, we can find our ground – eventually. Walking helps; breathing, too. Any rhythmic movement – however subtle – can help us settle. And so space can teach us how to rest and how to wait.

A meaningful life is not measured by a full calendar. We all know this. But we also easily forget that we can choose to live differently.

If you know you need breathing space, you have to be intentional about creating it. Today and next week and next year, long after you've read this book, you will need to remind yourself that you deserve breathing space and that you actually need it in order to remain who you actually are: a thinking, creative, connected human. You may even need to schedule it in your diary or put a sticky note on your laptop – reminding you to let your brain breathe: to go outside, have a nap, tend to yourself.

CREATE SOME GAPS

Look at this page. See the margins – the blank space on either side of the text. It gives you room to add notes – marginalia – but it also provides what author Elizabeth Strout refers to as 'the pragmatic helpfulness of white space on the page'. Imagine how heavy and inaccessible a page would feel if the text was squashed and blotted, extending from one corner to the other. Now consider what your schedule looks like. Have you created margins for pause, rest or contemplation? Where is the white space in your life?

FIVE WAYS TO …
Rest in the gaps

1. Intentionally soften your body each day. When you're busy, your body is moving quickly and is likely tense. When you deepen your breath and shake your limbs, you start to let go of tension; this is rest, and it can happen in the small gaps in your day.

2. Remind yourself that you're nature. Your energy, creativity and productivity are informed by the seasons. This is especially pertinent in winter: look at the trees, they're letting go of what's no longer needed, shedding the excess to make space for quiet rest. Sink into your own version of a slow winter.

3. Schedule breaks. Five minutes here, 20 minutes there, perhaps a whole hour or day. This is how you slow down, by giving it the same level of priority as work commitments and life appointments.

4. Move your awareness, in every spare moment, to the sky, a tree, the view from your window instead of picking up your phone. If you're not sure what to do in the space between everything else, go outside.

5. Sit in the silence and stillness instead of opting for distraction. Yes, it can be uncomfortable at first but, again, this is a habit that becomes easeful with practice. In the quiet, your brain takes a breather.

2

Befriend your vagus nerve

*Understanding our biology is a helpful step towards
prioritising ancient habits that support the body and
brain. When it comes to care, the vagus nerve is
in charge – it's the physiological pathway from
stress to calm.*

The vagus nerve is the caretaker of our nervous system, also
referred to in scientific studies as our 'sixth sense'. It's the
main component of the parasympathetic nervous system –
the easeful state of 'rest and digest' – and a constant assessor,
responding to the safety of a situation, the environment we're
in and the people we're with. Essentially, the vagus nerve
shapes how stressed we feel.

Dr Damian Holsinger, a senior lecturer in neuroscience at
the University of Sydney, emphasises that there's a lot we don't
know about it. 'We're still in the infancy of understanding how
the vagus nerve works,' he says. 'What happens when there are

high levels of cortisol and you stimulate the vagus nerve – you're kicking the parasympathetic nervous system into action, which overrides the cortisol and its activity on the nervous system.'

Vagus means wandering in Latin, and the name reflects the long pathway and extensive branching of the vagus nerve. It's the only cranial nerve that exits the brain and travels into the body, pervading every organ, all the way down to the gastrointestinal system. The gut–brain connection we've been hearing about? The vagus nerve is the conduit for that linkage.

Eradicating stress from your life is a fanciful ideal. It's not practical or helpful, and that's because stress is, sometimes, beneficial. Besides, many stressful events are outside of our control and our response to them is natural. But it's in these situations that awareness of your vagus nerve can really help. If you can be conscious of your stress and lean in to the practices that prompt activation of the parasympathetic nervous system, you're flexing your de-stress muscle. The more you use it, the more efficient it becomes.

TRAINING YOUR VAGUS NERVE

Getting to know this wandering nerve, and how best to activate it, is a tangible way of processing and minimising stress in the body. And that's because it's the main component of the parasympathetic nervous system, which is responsible for our heart rate, digestion and immune system – all involuntary. You can't control them, but you can strengthen your vagus nerve response and, by doing so, start to limit the biological impacts of stress. As Holsinger says, 'In periods of stress, the sympathetic nervous system is activated, which puts us in "fight or flight" mode. If you can activate your vagus nerve, you will feel calmer quicker and protect your body from the biological impacts of stress.'

On the flipside, if you're in a chronic state of stress, constantly striving without rest or space in between these high-stress bursts, your vagus nerve won't kick in. But as Holsinger says, if you activate your vagus nerve regularly, it will become a habit and, with practice, you'll be short-circuiting the switch between sympathetic and parasympathetic nervous system, between stress and breathing space.

'Each time you do something repeatedly, you're creating a circuit,' Holsinger says. 'We call it muscle memory, but it's actually a pathway you're creating, and when it's strengthened, the reaction time starts decreasing. Think of an Olympic athlete – they practise for hours on end to react to the starting gun. The more they do that, they're shortening their response to the starting gun. This is basically what we're doing – creating circuits in the system that shorten our reaction time. It's almost a reflex if you think about it.'

When we talk about habits to create space – intentionally resting, breathing deeply, swimming in cold water – we're actually reminding our vagus nerve that we're safe, and this helps us feel settled. The longer you practise these techniques, the longer your vagus nerve stays activated and the stronger your 'rest and digest' pathway becomes, so that it's easier to return to that state from a place of stress. This is relatively new science, and yet the research supports the benefits of ancient habits that directly support the parasympathetic nervous system.

A quick google search on the vagus nerve presents a slew of allied health practitioners discussing it. As Holsinger explains: 'The reason you go to any allied health practitioner is because there's something wrong with your body. And what we know about the vagus nerve is that it's a quick way of bringing the body back to balance.'

This doesn't mean that your autonomic nervous system is leaning more towards the parasympathetic; it means there's an even keel between both systems, so you're feeling grounded but can also respond to stress if needed. Of course, this takes time; these things can't be rushed. And while we have an element of control, and can check in with ourselves daily to promote a sense of ease, there will inevitably be stress in our lives.

Breathing space is *nervous system regulation.*

A well-trained vagus nerve is said to have high vagal tone, which is associated with improved health and better emotional and cognitive functioning. But what the nervous system loves is the familiar. And that's because the pathways we've created in the brain are comfortable – we know them, so they're an easier route to take. It's also why changing habits is hard and requires both intention and consistent practice. Our nervous system will respond in ways it always has unless we make intentional, consistent change. And that can begin with an awareness of our vagus nerve. Familiar feels safe, anything new feels uncertain.

But also, breathing space *is* nervous system regulation. Just sitting on the couch, comfortable and cosy, reading a book or watching comfort television is a form of essential care. As is recognising and acknowledging your exhaustion. Instead of pushing it down by pushing through, can you sit comfortably in your tiredness?

FIVE WAYS TO ...
Activate your vagus nerve

The vagus nerve responds to safety signals. Gentle daily nudges in the form of feel-good practices are familiar to the nervous system, telling it we're safe. Research confirms the profound connection between body and mind: bodily feedback has an extensive effect on our mental state, as 80 per cent of vagus nerve fibres transmit messages from body to brain. To create space in our mind, we must slow down our body. And just as we need to use our muscles regularly to ensure they're functioning optimally, we have to exercise our vagus nerve.

The five practices listed below and in the following pages aren't long or difficult, and don't require special equipment; they are available to you right now, right where you are. What is required is a shift in your mindset – the ability to pay attention to your body, acknowledge that you're feeling anxious and overwhelmed (it helps to say it out loud) and respond by reaching for these practices, leaning on them so you can settle your nervous system. When you do, you're creating moments of breathing space. The more you practise and the longer you can stay in the space you've created, the longer your vagus nerve will stay activated.

1. Cold water. It's okay, you don't need to hop in an ice bath. But immersing yourself in cold water can help slow your heart rate and redirect blood flow to your brain, essentially clearing your mind. The jolt of the cold – the forced discomfort – helps stimulate vagus nerve pathways and reduce the body's natural stress response.

Research shows that men and women respond differently to cold-water immersion, with some sources suggesting that ice baths aren't suitable for women's hormonal health. However, a recent study on cold-water swimming showed significant improvement in anxiety, mood swings, low mood and hot flushes in perimenopausal women. The key is to pay attention to how your body responds and be comforted by the fact that even small, quick experiences of cold are beneficial. You can apply the same method with an ice cube pressed into your neck, immersing your face in ice cold water for 10 seconds or turning off the hot tap at the end of your shower and letting the cold wash over you for 30 seconds, lengthening the time with each shower.

2. Deep, slow breathing. Just a few minutes of deep breathing can keep your vagus nerve active. Breathe in through your nose for a count of four and out through your mouth for a count of six. You can close your eyes if you feel like you need to focus, or watch your belly expand on the inhalation and contract on the exhalation. If your mind is wandering, mentally repeat: *I am breathing in, I am breathing out.*

Diaphragmatic breathing is another slow and simple form of breathwork (not breath control) that is proven to increase comfort, relaxation and alertness. It's best practised in a supine position (on your back) with one hand on your chest and the other on your belly as you breathe slowly and deeply through your nose to activate your vagus nerve. Ideally, only the hand on your belly is moving in rhythm with your breath.

3. Horizon gazing. When we're stressed, our field of vision narrows so one thing is in sharp focus and everything else is blurry. Expanding your visual field – letting your gaze be soft as you focus on the horizon, or letting your eyes wander from one thing to another in an open, green space – can effectively turn off your stress response. This shift in view also informs a shift in perspective: small problems don't feel so cumbersome when you're reminded of the big world around you. If you're stuck inside at your desk, keep your head neutral and move your gaze to one side, holding it until you sigh, then turn your eyes to the other side.

4. Loosen your jaw, relax your mouth, make low sounds. If you're stressed, chances are your breath is shallow and your jaw is tense. Any practice that loosens this tension is beneficial. The vagus nerve is connected to the vocal cords at the back of the throat, so when they're stimulated, they activate the vagus nerve. Gargling water, chanting om, humming or singing can all work.

5. Massage your neck and shoulders to release tension. We know that massage feels good, but studies show that head and neck massage can stimulate the vagus nerve, improving vagal tone and therefore activating the parasympathetic nervous system. Self-massage is beneficial, as is any yoga practice that focuses on releasing shoulder and neck tension.

3

Find your best forms of rest

Rest is subjective, so it's helpful to figure out what it looks like for you.

When you're told to rest, you may not know exactly what that means. It is a skill we've lost and one we need to return to because it protects the body and mind. We need to reinstate gentle pockets of downtime: take a breather, lie down for a nap, switch off the screens, consciously be offline.

Rest does not fit into a neat timeframe, nor does it look a certain way; it's subjective, vaguely defined and also often confused with sleep. It's for this reason that direct orders to rest feel confusing for a lot of people. We also live in a time where we socially dismiss the benefits of short rests, bitsy moments of downtime. And that's again because it looks like 'nothing' and is easily considered lazy or an inconsiderate waste of good time. This is a deeply ingrained belief for many people, who will exclaim that they couldn't possibly lie down on the bed in the middle of the day.

Be encouraged by the fact that rest can work in any context; you just have to figure out how it works for you. What exhausts you? What regenerates you? This is how you get to know yourself and the form of rest you intuitively need.

How you rest will likely change in response to where you are in life. The hormonal cycles of men and women are wildly different. Men exist in a 24-hour cycle, while women live in a monthly cycle, where the distinct shift in hormones informs an ebb and flow of energy, mood and mental clarity. The outer seasons will also dictate our rest habits.

The first step to integrating rest into your life is figuring out what rest looks like for you. This will be informed by your neurotype and your physical and mental health. It will also be determined by your life season, your work and caring responsibilities, and the time of year. Winter is dormant, and if we want to live in tune with nature, we must learn to observe lower energy levels and a call to curl up and rest in the dark so we have renewed energy when the light returns.

You don't need to be sick to slow down.

DEEP REST

Psychologist Dr Elissa Epel's studies support the idea of an easeful existence for long-term health and wellbeing, but she points out that our chronic stress is actually chronic uncertainty. The most practical first step? Get real about stress as a persistent part of life – it's not going anywhere. It's helpful to see it as normal and, sometimes, useful. A life without stress would be lacklustre; we would have no motivation. Instead of spending our time trying to eradicate it – and inevitably failing – perhaps we need to focus our attention on counterbalancing it. So what's a practical step forward for a less stressful, more easeful existence? Conscious and considered breathing space.

This is what Epel and her colleague Dr Alexandra Crosswell call 'deep rest'. Their scientific study supports what humans intuitively know: when we breathe deeply, walk in nature, potter around the home or let our mind wander in open space, it *feels* good, like we are, essentially, taking care of our deepest, truest self.

'Deep rest' may be a modern moniker but it is more than a trend. It's a long-established practice harking back centuries: the biblical sabbath, the meditation of ascetics, the work *and* rest of monks. It's nothing new. And so a return to ancient ways of living – at least in part – may be helpful to counterbalance the persistent hustle we find ourselves in.

Running through life feels so strained because we are the only mammals living this way. And yes, we think and analyse, create and critique, but on a primal level we can only flourish if we surrender to fallow periods. When we have time for our mind to rest – when we procrastinate, daydream, meander and play – we are laying fertile ground for ideas, growth and progress. In Christianity, there is the Sabbath. A friend who is also a pastor tells me that the seventh day is for rest, but the seventh hour in your day can be your reprieve, too.

How much deep rest do we need?

'We don't know the critical amount of deep rest, but we do know that even two minutes of slow breathing changes our physiology and our mood,' says Epel. 'So every minute is beneficial. Probably long periods, like a 90-minute yoga session that emphasises savasana – corpse pose [see page 100] – is a good dose of deep rest.'

Epel admits that there are seasons of life when rest is difficult to prioritise. 'In midlife, rest is a habit that's largely missing from our daily routine,' she says. 'It may come back during retirement, but by then we have had some irreversible ageing. Deep rest gives us the time to restore and repair on a daily basis or at least weekly.'

Habitual rest doesn't mean a sedentary life

It's important to note that deep rest doesn't mean that a life with little to no activity is beneficial. Ceasing to be active and engaged in life is detrimental to longevity and physiological and psychological wellbeing. Moments of intentional rest in the midst of a busy life are where the balance exists. We are more likely to live a full, long life if we prioritise breathing space.

How to find deep rest

Deep rest gives us the time to restore and repair on a daily basis. But first, we must reset. Epel suggests the following:

1. **Reset** *with two minutes of deep, conscious breathing.*
2. **Rest** *with a 30-minute yogic sleep, aka yoga nidra or savasana (see page 100).*
3. **Restore** *with intentional moments of downtime.*
4. **Repair** *by making deep rest habitual.*

You can rest right now, if you want to, but it's a decision you have to make for yourself – no one else can do it for you. Your body will force you if you reach a state of burnout, and that's not exactly ideal and it most definitely isn't convenient. Some health studies suggest that burnout, particularly workplace burnout, is not something you will necessarily fully recover from either. One scientific literature review shows that 25–50 per cent of people with clinical burnout do not make a full recovery four years after illness, and report greater exhaustion, less attentiveness, lower motivation, reduced work capability, and more negative health symptoms compared to their pre-burnout experience.

Ask anyone who has reached the point of not being able to get out of bed because they've got literally nothing left to give, and they'll tell you they regret not listening to the niggles and aches and exhaustion that persisted and eventually compounded, sending them off to hibernate for the foreseeable future. You can surrender when you've got no choice, or you can actively surrender when your body gives you warning signals. From both experiences you can learn to value rest, and connect it with a productive, sustainable, life moving forward (even if that life looks different from the one you're accustomed to). If you're a parent, this is one way of teaching your children how to care for themselves. When you model rest over doing, you're saying that this is an essential part of healthy living. In modern life, this ancient habit is actually a necessary life skill. It's one we need to learn, practise and hone … and then teach so that it is normalised.

It's something you should be doing every day, regardless of your plans. In fact, sometimes planning rest – scheduling it into your week – is the best way to integrate it into your days, setting the foundation so it becomes a habit. You can start right now, if you want to. There's no 'right' way to do this, there's no external measurement for 'enough' rest; it's very much an individual thing. But by doing it regularly you'll come to realise and value the physical, emotional and mental benefits. *Rest is space.*

Just as artists and writers often lament the lack of time to create, many of us do the same with rest. We like to grasp minutes and hold tight to hours, but letting go a little is often a good thing. Loosen your grip on time and you're entering a more restful state of being.

Say no without the 'I'm too busy' excuse

If you want to shift the cultural narrative around rest, start talking about it. This means deprioritising 'busy' as a status symbol (and an excuse) and being honest about your need for rest. If a friend asks you to catch up or if you need to cancel a social event, state the facts: 'I'm tired and I really need to lie low and take care of myself.'

The busier we are, the more we need rest

Rest is usually the first thing we drop when life and everything in it feels urgent. This is actually one of the very early symptoms of burning out – the sense that you can't stop because if you do, nothing will get done. Time suddenly feels scarce – there's a very real (to you) sense that it's running out. And so you drop what's least urgent – rest, home cooking, exercise, socialising – and soothe yourself with quick fixes that essentially make you feel worse: doom scrolling, alcohol, takeaway, caffeine, sugar. It feels like shallow breaths and tense limbs, a frantic moving from one task to the next as you scramble to complete them all, protecting and guarding your time above all else, fretting that it's vanishing and you're not working fast enough, hard enough – enough! Fuelled by a constantly elevating adrenaline rush, all of your awareness is in your head – thumping energy and scattered thoughts that rush. There's no ease to the process; everything seems hurried and harried because *it feels like you're running out of time.*

But what if space – and rest – gave you time? It's not as if suddenly whole hours will appear in front of you, but you can shift your perspective and place limitations on your day. Be mindful of yourself and your minutes, dedicate yourself to using 25 minutes wisely and well – with intention and focus. This isn't about segmenting your days into 25-minute bursts of activity but about learning the mental benefits of compartmentalising. And if you can do it with work, you can do it with rest, too.

SAVASANA

I spent many years watching people breathe. As a yoga teacher, I would instruct my students to gather all their thoughts and awareness concerned with *out there* and bring them back to *in here*. I watched jaws unclench and shoulders drop and a sense of softening settle into their bodies. Bellies held tight suddenly relaxed and all the pent-up tension, evident in furrowed brows and creaky hips loosened, and was often released in tears or, sometimes, uncontrollable laughter.

I'm sure that most students came to my classes for the yoga nidra practice at the end. Some even admitted to me that they begrudgingly stretched and bent just to get the opportunity to lie down and do nothing afterwards. But the 'nothing' they were talking about is what Epel calls one of the most powerful forms of 'deep rest'. Yoga nidra, or yogic sleep, is a guided meditation, and some sources claim that the 30–60-minute practice is equivalent to three to four hours of sleep. The positive effects on the central nervous system have been objectively measured, with neuroimaging studies showing yoga nidra produces changes in dopamine release and blood flow to the brain, and may reduce symptoms of mild depression and anxiety.

Yoga nidra definitely feels like a deep form of rest – it's slightly different from both sleep and relaxation, and some sources refer to it as a 'third mental state'. When someone is telling you to *let go* and *lie heavy* in savasana – corpse pose – you're very much doing your best to play dead and let the earth hold all your weight. You're coming back to yourself, coming back home.

It begins with the encouragement to wriggle and stretch your body – release any obvious tension – and then take three deeper-than-normal inhalations followed by big, releasing sighs before your body becomes still and gradually settles, and your awareness is guided around your body. You're not supposed to fall asleep but to exist in that sweet spot just before it. The air is even still when a room of people are sinking into deep quiet. Sometimes the 'letting go' involves a limb lifting up and falling back down again, soft tears.

If you can't nap during the day and you find it hard to wind down at night, listening to a yoga nidra can be a practical way of settling yourself. It may take you a few practices to feel comfortable. Your mind will likely wander, especially if you're feeling overwhelmed by a busy brain. Try not to judge yourself; switching off and letting go even when you're being guided by an external voice doesn't always come easily. But with consistency, you'll gradually slip into the practice quicker and with less resistance.

FIVE FORMS OF …
Rest

Remember that rest is simply an absence of effort – doing nothing, but also doing something that doesn't require anything of you. Active rest looks like:

1. Social rest. Spending time with people who bolster you with meaningful conversation and thoughtful questions, people who listen without interruption or judgement.

2. Mental rest. Journalling to process your thoughts, walking to let your jumbled thoughts dissipate, repeating mantras to regulate your emotions.

3. Sensory rest. Soothing your nervous system by embracing comforts like a warm bath, an early night, dim lights, nourishing food, a hot drink, rhythmic music.

4. Physical rest. Releasing tension and stress in your body with things like swimming, stretching, dancing, massage or yoga. Or lying like a starfish on your bed and breathing deep into your belly.

5. Emotional rest. Processing your thoughts with someone you trust, letting go of what's bothering you to make sense of persistent worries.

4

Honour the season you're in

We are nature and we live in response to cyclical rhythms. This is ancient knowledge and it's precisely what we need to guide us through modern life if we want to live well. Seasons help us connect to the natural world; they're the incentive we need to give our brain space to rest, mull and wander.

Chronobiology is the biology of cycles in living things. Every organism on earth – ourselves included – exists and adapts in response to solar and lunar cycles and their rhythms, which dictate light, seasons and tides.

We are nature and nature is always changing. There is some comfort in reminding ourselves of this constant change, even if it's subtle. Our body is never stagnant, and neither is the natural world. And for all the remedies and products that promise to 'fix' our ailments, this simple biological fact is the answer to our discomfort, exhaustion and numbness. We've become separated from the natural rhythms of our body and the earth, but that doesn't mean we can't make our way back to the ancient habit of acknowledging the rhythm and living in tune with it. So much of our overwhelmed feeling is actually misalignment because we exist in an engineered world that effectively ignores the fact that we are natural beings.

It might seem a bit far-fetched, but every cell in our body has its own biological clock that correlates to the rhythms of the earth, the sun and the moon. Nearly every tissue and organ within the body has its own circadian rhythm, and collectively they are tuned to the daily cycle of night and day.

Our 'master' clock, which regulates time and controls our rhythms, is located in the brain. It's a large group of nerve cells that form a structure called the suprachiasmatic nucleus (SCN), which produces the hormone melatonin in response to the amount of light our eyes receive. This is why seeking direct sunlight after waking in the morning is one of the best things you can do to improve your sleep at night; the UV feeds into your brain to kickstart the production of melatonin that will make you sleepy once it's dark. Of course, once it's dark we are bathed in the light of the screens that hold our attention and keep us awake, preventing the release of melatonin. But if you follow the advice of the world's sleep experts and switch off screens in the evening – not a difficult task – you're taking a small but deeply significant step towards settled sleep, which is the most powerful form of rest for your body and your brain.

Ask yourself two questions when you wake each morning:

1. *How am I feeling?*
2. *What do I need?*

This is how you nurture self-awareness.

WE ARE NATURAL BEINGS WITH NATURAL RHYTHMS

A world that always expects us to be 'on' and that doesn't necessarily encourage any 'off' time, also prevents us from moving in tune with biologically normal rhythms. This is having a profound impact on our capacity to be well and perform well. We can try all we want, but we can't be healthy and not also acknowledge our humanity – the fact that first and foremost we're nature, and our existence and energy are informed by the cycles and seasons we observe out the window.

In nature, diversity is the root of strength and resilience. As we age, it's these two traits that defend us against chaos and whim. Despite our thinking brains that dream, critique and analyse, we are animals, and all creatures exist in periods of ebb and flow – activity and receptivity. Our brains are commonly said to have evolved for life 10,000 years ago (when we were already 95 per cent of the way along our evolutionary timeline), so they're not designed or equipped for modern life, but they do respond to ancient cycles – seasonal, lunar and tidal. And when we understand the body and brain, we are more likely to lean in to these cycles and allow ourselves to exist in response to them. This existence is soft and quiet; it encourages us to reach for comfort in habits that don't require any effort.

If we apply a hormonal lens, this means that in a world fuelled by the stress hormone cortisol we're leaning in to the healing, restoring power of oxytocin, the 'cuddle chemical' that makes us feel cosy. It's a life with fewer screens and more paper pages, dim lamps instead of overhead fluorescents, an afternoon nap instead of pushing through, and being okay with what is instead of always striving for bigger and better. The repercussions of this conscious low-effort softening is a sharper mind and a more resilient body: wellbeing.

The slow-lifestyle movement that has gained traction in the past few decades is an expected response to a life that is propelling us forwards in great leaps and ungainly bursts. But it also feels unattainable for so many of us, even if we understand that it's a positive choice for wellbeing.

90 minutes' work / 20 minutes' rest

How often should we stop work to rest so we increase productivity and reduce fatigue? If we leave behind the stultifying effects of schedules and routines and consider rhythm, ideally we should work for no longer than 90 minutes before taking a break. Consider it a recharge of the body's batteries; we are designed to have periods of intermittent rest throughout each day. We even have an inbuilt system dictating this recurrent cycle of alternating high-frequency (work) and low-frequency (rest) brain activity. It's called the ultradian rhythm, and when we can get in sync with it, we're more likely to be productive when we work. This is because periods of high brain activity – when we're alert and focused – are dependent on intentional periods of rest. After about 90 minutes of work, the telltale signs that your brain activity is slowing down are likely there: yawning, being easily distracted, hunger. Your body is already winding down because *it needs rest* before it can switch into work mode again, and it will do this for about 20 minutes.

You can observe these changes to your brain, take note and rest so your brain can renew. Or you can ignore them and push through. 'Pushing through' may seem, on the surface, to be the most productive choice, but it's actually pushing your brain to its limits – and the result is increased stress, less focus and the tendency to make mistakes. If you want to avoid feeling exhausted and depleted at the end of every day, take regular breaks where you actively step away from your work and observe 20 minutes of intentional downtime.

Ebb and flow is a natural part of life

When we live according to our cycle, we don't need as much rest because we're living in tune with what our body needs. We don't reach the point of exhaustion because we don't push ourselves that far. We're not the same every day, so how we rest will change. And yet this inner truth is often lost because we're busy all the time, and when 'busy' is the normal pace, we don't have the opportunity to follow life's rhythms. Socrates is said to have warned of the barrenness of a busy life, and if I think about it long enough I can see his point: a full schedule doesn't allow for a change of pace. The consistent demands keep us pushing through.

The only certainty is that things will change. Real life is a constant flow of energy – pushing and pulling us along. Sometimes the energy halts and we do, too. At certain times it spirals – usually in liminal periods of change when we have to wait to know what direction we're heading in next. We crave the stability of the predictable, but the normal state of things is flow, disruption, surprise. The uncertainty of this can rattle us, and yet we frequently dismiss our internal weather system, which is largely a consistent measure of energy.

We often look at the external weather forecast to see what it will bring and we plan accordingly. We can do that with our own cycles, too.

THE MENSTRUAL CYCLE

Madeleine Murray is a midwife and cycle educator who teaches women about the physiological and emotional phases of the menstrual cycle. She believes there are several reasons we've drifted away from this ancient knowledge, the most pertinent being that we're living in a world geared to the 24-hour male hormonal cycle, one that's championed by consistency and productivity and therefore reliant on stability of energy. The consequences of this are evident in all the women I know: a profound exhaustion and abject weariness. Why? We've been conditioned to suppress our inner ebb and flow of energy and instead try to maintain a pace that is energetically detrimental.

'It's pushing women to maintain the same consistency, energy, productivity and presence every single day of the month, which simply isn't aligned with our monthly hormonal cycle,' Murray says. 'I believe the impact of this disconnection is profound. I think women's mental health would improve significantly if we acknowledged the cycle – the ebb and flow and push and pull of energy, the ups and the downs of mood, rather than commonly feeling guilty when we are in lower-energy phases wondering why we can't keep up.'

This feeling of not doing or not being 'good enough' plagues women. It can prompt a really debilitating sense of both guilt and shame that can and often does inform anxiety and depression. It's important to note that most scientific studies on the body have only ever been done on men. Women's health is just starting to be acknowledged by science, thanks to women demanding answers.

Our hormonal seasons

Many people quickly dismiss this awareness of menstrual cycles as woo-woo when it's actually a simple biological process. We can beautify it or we can choose to view it through a hormonal lens. The rise and fall of hormones over a monthly cycle informs a distinct shift in energy, mood and mindset, which in turn affects our creativity and productivity. We see the same patterns in nature, particularly in places where the seasons are distinct:

- **Winter** *is sparse and bare, and requires warmth and nourishment in the form of rest – a hibernation of sorts.*
- **Spring** *has an undeniable sense of optimism as colour returns and plants shoot up and out with renewed energy.*
- **Summer** *is energetic and also languid; outward energy is abundant and we feel innately generous.*
- **Autumn** *is a stripping bare, a closing-in and falling of energy as we start to huddle.*

The four seasons and their characteristics can be used to describe the phases of the menstrual cycle, which are dictated by oestrogen, progesterone, follicle-stimulating hormone (FSH) and luteinising hormone.

When we intentionally choose to rest in inner winter (when we're menstruating, our hormones are at their lowest and our energy is depleted), we're creating space for our body to focus on bleeding (loss of blood means the body needs warmth and rest to rejuvenate) and allowing our energy to naturally rebuild for the outward-focused phases ahead.

These phases – inner spring and summer when oestrogen is rising – are ripe for creativity and productivity, because we have the energy to invest in getting things done (and a bit of testosterone aids this process). But there's no set time for each person with a cycle; it's far more nuanced than that. All humans are unique, and cyclical living requires, first and foremost, the cultivation of self-awareness. Rather than follow a predetermined plan, we need to tune in and get to know our own inner cycle.

'It's not about having another set of rules to follow or a structure,' Murray says. 'I feel like people can get attached to these four phases in a limiting way, which can lead to pre-empting or anticipating the struggles or challenges, which is absolutely not what cyclical living is about. Instead, it's about honing an awareness of your needs and living in alignment with that. This requires some flexibility.'

That's the crux of cyclical living: the ability to pivot and the grace to accept change. Murray suggests experimenting and observing; it's how you get to know yourself. 'Experiment with consciously slowing down during your inner autumn and resting during your inner winter, and then observe what happens during the ovulatory phase [inner summer],' she says. 'It's important to play with it – push through a cycle when you bleed and observe how you feel for the rest of the month; rest one cycle and see what happens in ovulation. Don't let me or anyone say, "You're productive here, you're creative here, you're going to be depressed here." Instead, pay attention and take note. Cyclical living is about increasing self-awareness, being more reflective and living in line with your needs, which are innately rhythmic.'

British psychoanalyst Marion Milner documented her reflections on 'the basic problems with living' in her diaries that extended over decades – an early form of self-help. In her nine books, she explored themes of leisure and creativity – essentially what to do with her 'free time'.

In her 1937 book *An Experiment in Leisure*, she writes: 'knowing what you really want is an exceedingly delicate process: to bridge the gap between vague inner urgencies and the practical possibilities of the outer world requires the finest co-ordination and economy of mental power'. This mental power is actually self-awareness and discipline; to let your body be the guide and turn away from social expectations. And it's really hard! But abundant leisure time – rest, socialising, play – has been the norm for 95 per cent of human history; it has always been sacrosanct in hunter-gatherer societies. And while the transition from foraging to farming was considered progressive, it significantly changed how much we worked, resulting in a marked reduction in leisure time, especially for women. Leisure time and engaging in soothing practices (handiwork and hobbies) gives the brain a rest from scanning for threats. It's healthy stimulation that helps the brain create new neural pathways.

We cannot change the modern world, but we can choose to honour our need for rest in small ways (life still happens and we need to continue with our work life and parenting/ caring responsibilities). In doing so, we create the opportunity to access the strengths of each phase, particularly inner spring and summer – the follicular and ovulatory phases. And if you don't clock the need to rest or you have to push through? There's a very real likelihood that for the remainder of the month you'll feel a bit behind energetically, or like you're playing catch-up. Perhaps you won't feel as much in your creative and productive power because you don't have the stamina or mental clarity to get you to where you're at

your brightest. Some months this realisation may be overt –
a distinct connection between the rest you take in inner
winter and the bright potential and power of inner summer.
And other times it's more subtle, particularly in demanding
seasons where all the outer obligations impinge.

Cyclical living stems from a physiological and emotional
awareness of each phase and the intention to shift your daily
rhythms accordingly. In modern life, this is rarely a seamless
process. Some months it just isn't possible – but also, it doesn't
require massive change. During inner winter in particular,
small choices have a meaningful impact: resting in the gaps
between, choosing the easy option for dinner, prioritising an
early night, having more self-compassion for your low energy
and motivation.

The reasons we've drifted away from feminine awareness
are complex. While the early waves of feminism were crucial
for female rights, they focused on matching male capabilities
rather than celebrating or even acknowledging our unique
rhythms and strengths. The widespread use of hormonal
contraception was revolutionary for women's autonomy, but
it does mask our natural cycle. These are both contributing
factors to our disconnection from our cyclic nature, and it nods
to the inherent gap between ancient ways of being and the
demands of modern life.

What we do have control over is how we bridge that gap,
acknowledging and listening to our biology and figuring
out how we can live seasonally and cyclically. Sometimes
everything will flow, other times it may feel a bit disjointed,
but there is profound contentment in simply being aware
and, ultimately, re-establishing our connection to a cycle that
explains so much about who we are and how we move through
the world. Murray agrees: 'I think women's mental health

would improve significantly if we acknowledged the cycle – the ebb and flow and push and pull of it, the ups and the downs, rather than feeling guilt when we're in lower, downward-energy phases. I think women access more of their creativity when living cyclically. We feel more connected with our deeper self, which I believe leads to living a more content, reflective and connected life.'

Honour the life season you're in

We live according to life seasons. It's helpful to acknowledge that there's a lot we can control about our days but we do so in light of where we're at: moving house, tertiary study, early parenthood, a new career, illness, divorce, parenting teenagers. Sometimes these seasons are short and sometimes they persist, but they are always informed by our internal season (our menstrual cycle, pregnancy, lactation, perimenopause) and the external season (summer, autumn, winter, spring). I call this *honouring the season you're in*. While it's normal to want to resist the limitations this season creates for us, it's much more helpful to accept that this is where we're at and make decisions accordingly. I find it deeply comforting to recognise my waning energy and understand that it's normal considering where I'm at in my cycle (low energy, post-ovulation).

Once you recognise the season you're in, start practising a whole lot of self-compassion. Because when you lower your ideals, appreciate your strengths and acknowledge your vulnerabilities, you start to go easy on yourself, which means you create more space. It's a surrender of sorts, an acceptance of who you are and where you're at. It feels like a sweet exhale, a big shoulder drop – permission to go at your own pace. I think this is one way to take care of yourself.

Living in sync with the rhythm of life is how we've always lived. Never before have we been as hurried and harried as we are now, and many of us, whether we're aware of it or not, have adopted a robotic routine that inhibits our body's regular calls for rest. We keep going and going until we crash. We rest (inconveniently) and then pick up the pace. There's no down time; we're not taking a breather.

TUNE IN

The first step towards making space is to develop the ancient habit of paying attention to what your body is telling you. This starts with the simple act of checking in with yourself each day. We often forget that our body tells us what we need, because stress and distraction override this inbuilt messaging system. Remember, your body is wise – it knows exactly what it requires in order to feel energised and rested. Listen and it will tell you. Ask yourself three questions:

1. *How am I feeling?*
2. *What do I need?*
3. *How can I take care of myself?*

You don't have to know the answers, but the simple act of asking yourself these questions means you're paying attention to yourself. This is how you nurture your intuition. Think of it as the tiny voice within that, when you pay attention to it, can be a valuable tool – a moral guide. What gets in the way of it? Distraction, phones, social-media comparison. The panopticon of social media – of being watched but also being influenced – erodes our sense of self because we're often in comparison mode, and this makes us question who we are and what we like. If rest is an act of resistance, simply sitting with yourself without distraction is, too. It's helpful to remember that what your body needs isn't complicated, but it does require you to get out of your head and listen. When you're thirsty, drink water. When you're tired, lie down for 10 minutes. When you feel tension, stretch and move and dance.

Sometimes it can be helpful to stop and step to the side, but it's hard to stand still and contemplate while everyone rushes along ahead of you. This, however, is an opportunity to figure out what matters and then make choices that feel good because you're making them based on your own moral compass and not what's expected of you. You may be still but you're not stagnant. Hope, Rebecca Solnit writes, is 'the belief that what we do matters even though how and when it may matter, who and what it may impact, are not things we can know beforehand'. Creating space in your life requires cultivation; you have to plant the idea and nurture it so it grows into something. Through a cyclical-living lens, these ideas germinate in inner winter and come to fruition in inner spring and summer.

FIVE THINGS TO ...
Do on low-energy days

1. Do one thing on your to-do list. Just one – no more. Today isn't about ambition, it's about being gentle and opting for what's most doable. If you can't even do one thing, that's fine. Most things can wait.

2. Choose the easy option. Convenience is there to carry you through the busy, sad, too-hard, exhausted weeks. Order takeaway, remember that eggs on toast is a fine choice for dinner, postpone what isn't necessary.

3. Go for a 10-minute walk in your comfies. Even when you don't really want to walk, it's helpful to remember that walking doesn't require 'exercise' gear. When you have little energy, a stroll can lighten your perspective.

4. Build a nest so you feel safe. Sometimes the root cause of our stress is feeling untethered – that all-at-sea feeling where you're not really sure when the next wave is going to hit. What you need most during these times is a sense of stability and security. You need to lean in to what gives you the most comfort: cradling a hot cup of tea, wearing your softest cotton, cuddling up on the couch to watch your favourite movie, retreating to bed with warm socks and a hot water bottle.

5. Step through a nourishing bedtime routine. Leave your phone in another room, have a warm shower or bath (this helps release oxytocin, the hormone that relaxes you), make tea, snuggle into the sheets, read a book.

5

Slow down and sidestep

When you recognise that you're swept up in a perpetual race for bigger and better, you may flail, unsure of which way to turn. Stop for a moment, take a step to the side, return to the basics and move at a human pace – this is how you care for yourself.

Part of modern exhaustion is a depletion of attention. We can't focus because we're distracted, which is stressful because when we can't apply our attention we become irritable and impatient. Decision-making is hard, problem-solving and creative productivity feel impossible. We lean further in, grasping for answers and solutions, willing them into being, and this is itself a stressful experience because we're waiting in anticipation for what comes next, desperate for progress. This dizzying way of living – usually fast, frantic and haphazard because it's engineered to be that way – is remedied by letting our brain breathe.

When life feels like a whirlwind, the only solution is
to return to the basics. And that starts by giving ourselves
permission. You are allowed to choose to care for yourself.
It's not something you need to earn, either. It's a requirement
for living well and that's a human right.

The first step is a reset – switching off for a few moments
so you can come back to everyday life with a clearer mind. And
the key to making sustainable change? A habit shift that starts
with intention and progresses to small, achievable changes. It
was, for me, the understanding of how my mind works – how
I write and create, yes, but also how to care for it, tend to it
like my body. It's knowing that when the fog descends, and
I procrastinate and distract myself instead of concentrating
on the problem at hand and sinking into a flow state, what
I need to do is step away. Move away to move forward, in a
sense. I think that may be why so many of us find it hard to
value and then make time for rest – or even something that
isn't 'work' – because it can feel like we're moving backwards.
That's why I like to reframe it as a step to the side, away from
the communal race and, sometimes, away from our own
expectations. In busy, pressing times, it's easier to let go of the
habits that nurture us than it is to hold onto them.

No, you can't escape normal life and work obligations, but
you can schedule the downtime and rest that allow you to lean
in to what you most need to stay well in busy periods. This isn't
about spending whole days in bed reading a really good book
(although if you have the opportunity to do this, please do –
it is one of the great pleasures in life) but about establishing
a better perspective.

It's also helpful to accept that there will be days when
nothing goes to plan, when you don't practise even the most
reliable habits or they don't provide their usual fortifying

benefits. This is normal life, which ebbs and flows, just like our energy levels, clarity and enthusiasm. A sidestep is about leaving toxic productivity culture behind, and with it the pressure to always tick the boxes and reach our self-imposed goals. Some days just don't unfold neatly and that's okay – it's not a failing, you don't have to carry guilt about your lack of ideal performance, you can just choose to be gentle with yourself and sink into the slower pace.

HOW TO TAKE A STEP TO THE SIDE

You may feel like a life with less stress is out of reach, but you don't have to look out there for the remedy. Breathing space isn't complicated. Make small changes by starting with one thing. This could be:

1. *sun*
2. *sleep*
3. *movement*
4. *breath*
5. *reading.*

Each of these can benefit your brain health and mental health. Here's how.

1. Sun

For all of time, life has been dictated by the sun. It prompts us to start and end the day, it boosts our immune system, and influences the seasons and our energy levels, which are naturally more robust in summer when the days are long and the sun is high, and generally more fallow in winter. When you get the sun on your face first thing in the morning, even if it's just for a few minutes, it reinforces your circadian rhythm and can help relieve the heaviness of sleep deprivation. It's your body's way of knowing that it's time to wake up and get moving and thinking. Seeking light in the morning helps you wind down at night, too.

2. Sleep

Sleep is the ultimate arbiter of our physical and emotional health. It makes everything better because it's the most powerful form of healing. When we sleep, our body relaxes and restores; renews energy; boosts our immunity; and repairs muscles, tissues, organs and cells. Sleep also allows our brain to process the day. Think of sleep as a form of mental decluttering as it sifts through thoughts, information and conversations. It's also inhibited by stress and influenced by life seasons (new parenthood and perimenopause, especially). Sleep deprivation is the tipping point to mental health conditions, which is why more sleep is the first prescription given by psychologists and psychiatrists after a diagnosis. Sleep is the most basic form of breathing space – a biological constant. It's an ancient habit we simply cannot avoid and should learn to honour, and we can do this by fostering bedtime rituals that are simple steps to settling but also gentle forms of care.

Gender also informs sleep quality. Women are more likely to experience sleep disturbances because female sex hormones – oestrogen and progesterone – affect the brain region that involves sleep regulation. During the first two weeks of the menstrual cycle, known as the follicular phase, when the body is flowing with oestrogen and progesterone is low, sleep is generally longer and more settled.

The importance of REM sleep

In rapid eye movement (REM) sleep three important things happen:

- **memory consolidation**. You're integrating everything you learnt that day.
- **physical repair**. Your body is fixing itself, whether you went to the gym and your muscles need repairing or your immune system needs strengthening.
- **emotional processing**. Your brain is consolidating positive emotions to your memory and weakening strong negative or traumatic emotions.

If over time you get less and less sleep, your body prioritises emotional processing over physical repair and memory consolidation and integration. So after a while you get sick. And what are you forced to do, even if it's inconvenient? Get into bed. Your body is smart; it almost always gets its way.

For many, sleep is elusive. If you're already exhausted and wired, or an over-thinker who finds it hard to wind down, falling asleep (and staying asleep) can be a challenge. This can further exacerbate your anxiety, which feeds your exhaustion. If you're in this cycle, recognise it and know that there are things that will help, mostly the knowledge that we are designed to sleep but not necessarily right through the night. Wakings are evolutionarily normal for babies and children especially, but there's also research that points to the ancient practice of 'two sleeps' and the benefits of this segmented rest for adults, too. Circadian rhythms affect our hormones, but this process is also bidirectional. There are prominent times in a woman's life in particular when hormones will inhibit good-quality sleep, namely pregnancy, postpartum, perimenopause and menopause. Women are nearly twice as likely to develop insomnia, whereas men have double the risk of developing sleep apnoea.

Professor Russell Foster, director of the Sleep and Circadian Neuroscience Institute at the University of Oxford, reiterates on the *Just One Thing* podcast, that a good night's sleep starts with how we spend our day and especially what we do when we wake up. The quality of our day – the light we get, how much we move, the food we eat and the amount of time we spend on screens – directly affects the quality of our sleep.

'We're used to thinking that the quality of our sleep defines the quality of our consciousness and awake state, but it's reciprocal,' Foster says. As well as being intentional with how you spend the first hour of your day, you may need to adopt a bedtime ritual of sorts – a series of steps to prepare you for sleep that when practised regularly become routine. Parents do it with their children because the ritual in itself is grounding. When we practise the same series of steps each evening, our body and mind are comforted by this habitual behaviour and it becomes automatic.

Creating a space conducive to sleep is important – it's a conscious and intentional closing of the day that allows our body and mind to slow and soften. In Chapter 11, I talk more about creating zones in your house for rest and work. Sometimes a sleep to-do list is comforting, but for some it can feel overwhelming. If this is you, doing just one sleep-promoting thing from this list is still meaningful:

- *Aim for the ideal room temperature for sleep, which is 18 degrees Celsius (64 degrees Fahrenheit).*
- *Go to bed at the same time each night to reinforce your circadian rhythm.*
- *Dim the lights in the evening to encourage melatonin (the hormone the brain releases in darkness to help you sleep).*
- *Switch screens off at least 30 minutes before sleep.*
- *Keep your bedroom a phone-free space. I started keeping my phone in the kitchen at night and purchased a dim digital clock (it only lights up if I hit the button) that sits on my bedside table.*
- *Wash away the day with a shower or a bath in dim light.*
- *Drink a 'sleep' herbal tea, such as chamomile.*
- *Read a book.*
- *Breathe in slowly for a count of four and exhale for a count of six.*

The first 30–90 minutes after waking is when your limbic system (your emotional brain) is more active and cortisol is naturally high (it is, in part, what wakes you). This means that your brain is more receptive to stimuli; it's in a highly dopamine-sensitive state.

If the first thing you do is scroll on your phone, you're immediately leaning in to stress, which is difficult to backtrack from. But what if you considered this time as gentle space to awaken, move and create?

3. Movement

You need to move your body to get your energy flowing. If you feel stagnant and lethargic, exhausted and slumpy, often the best remedy is to get your blood pumping. The same goes if you're feeling irritable and agitated – your body is telling you to let the energy go, there's too much built-up tension. Our bodies were designed to move, but that doesn't mean that you need to slip into a fitness or body-improvement mindset (so many of us recoil at this). Think of movement as an ancient way of taking care of yourself and then move intuitively. A gentle walk around your neighbourhood may be the best choice for you when you feel soft and vulnerable. When you feel exhausted and buzzy with too much adrenaline, pick up the pace and let the endorphins moderate your stress. Move in a way that feels good for you. While a walk is always a good idea, so is stretching or shaking your limbs.

4. Breath

Breathing is living, the most basic human function that requires none of our awareness. And yet you're immediately more aware of your breath – its length and quality – because you're reading about it. For more on breathwork and approaches you can take, see pages 38 and 90.

5. Reading

Sometimes it's helpful to escape your own life and venture into another, if only for a few moments. Reading helps us feel empathy, but it's also one of the most powerful forms of relaxation. I don't have to convince you of this, but I think it's encouraging to know the facts: a 2009 study showed that reading for six minutes can lower our stress levels by as much as 68 per cent – muscle tension eases and our heart rate slows.

It's more effective than drinking a hot cup of tea or going for a walk. It's why people say they can't finish their book because they only read a few pages before they fall asleep. Aha! Exactly! Reading is also one of the leading recommendations for insomnia and is encouraged as a relaxing bedtime ritual. It's relaxing because the concentration required has a physiological effect on the brain, which contributes to the winding-down of the sympathetic nervous system. As the stress hormones dissipate, the fear centre of the brain becomes less active and the parts of the brain involved in language, social cognition, memory and concentration light up. Your brain is working hard but you feel calmer.

Bibliotherapy – the therapeutic practice of reading to support mental health – can be traced back to Ancient Greece, where libraries were considered 'healing places of the soul'. It has physiological benefits, too. Researchers at Yale University's School of Public Health found that reading books can essentially give us a survival advantage. Their results suggest that reading literally lengthens our life: a 20 per cent reduction in mortality was observed for those who read books, compared to those who did not.

Reading is a circuit breaker for modern-life rumination because, as well as reducing stress, it stimulates synapses in the frontal lobe – the part of the brain that controls attention and executive function. A recent study by the Queen's Reading Room in collaboration with pioneering neuroscience research shows that as well as helping us wind down, reading fiction can improve focus and concentration. You don't have to dedicate whole hours to your book. Short bursts of five minutes immersed in a novel have profound benefits for your brain, including:

- **An immediate reduction in stress**. *Reading interrupts overwhelming thought cycles in our brain and reduces cortisol.*
- **Better management of stress**. *You're less likely to feel stressed while thinking about everyday challenges and, therefore, you navigate them with more ease.*
- **Increased ability to concentrate**. *Reading changes the connections in the brain and the way these connections (also known as synapses) talk to each other, which can improve your ability to focus. But also, when you're reading, you're actively practising focus and concentration and the ability to avoid distraction.*

Reading fiction can also alleviate the isolation of modern life by decreasing feelings of loneliness and increasing empathy, because with the characters we come to know, we experience a sense of belonging and feel more connected to others. Reading makes us more empathetic humans. And at a time when our language and literacy skills are in sharp decline, we need the fortifying benefits of books and we need to model reading to our children, who are growing up in a hyper-artificial world. Have books in your home, carry a paperback in your bag, join your local library and visit weekly; this is how you integrate reading into your life.

START THE DAY WITH SPACE

Three mornings a week I wake in the dark, well before dawn, and walk straight to the kitchen to boil the kettle. I can see the church, the cross lit, and the sea from there, and I look out for the two minutes it takes for the water to boil. I'm usually tired, but I've been doing this long enough to understand how precious this hour is, before I am inevitably drawn to the obligatory lunchbox packing and corralling of children from beds. In these quiet hours, I can be soft with myself, and attend to the words that need to be written and that seem to flow seamlessly at this hour before my critical mind has woken. I may be romanticising my life, but this is a good thing because it promotes mindfulness, which decreases anxiety, rumination and emotional reactivity.

This idea of starting the day with space has changed so much for me. There is a clarity that comes from uninterrupted writing time before anything else in the day, before I'm distracted or needed elsewhere, and I now protect it because it dictates my mindset. Even if the words are clunky or few, the opportunity to sit at the desk and be ... before anything else, before anyone else ... that's enough, that's the space I need.

FIVE WAYS TO …
Start the day with more space

1. Don't leap out of bed. Instead, take a few deep breaths, stretch your body in a way that feels good, and check in with how you're feeling. If you notice you're particularly tired, make rest a priority later in the day.

2. Move slowly and intentionally. Make a cup of tea, potter in the kitchen, look out the window.

3. Let your mind wander. It's still waking up, so let it be soft for as long as possible (resisting screens is one way to do this).

4. Write your dreams, thoughts and ideas on paper. It may also help to write down what you need to do for the day, starting with the next most necessary thing.

5. Go outside and turn your face to the sun, go for a wander. Being outside in the early morning, through the seasons, allows you to be with the world as it wakes up, too.

You don't have to do all of these things in one morning; you may only do one or two. But they're worthwhile, even though each step takes just a few minutes.

6
Check your habits

Creating a new normal is dependent on establishing the right habits for you. Think of them as foundational steps for brain health – they're non-negotiable in a world that consumes our attention and clutters the mind.

We are living in an age of information overload where we are effectively gorging on facts, stats, advice and rhetoric. Whatever lives 'rent-free' in your mind is actually costing you breathing space, because while we know how to gather information, we haven't yet honed the ability to sift through it, taking only what we need. This isn't something to feel guilty about. Instead, it's helpful to remember that the brain is instinctively seeking new information because it's designed for the simple existence of 10,000 years ago when 'new' was rare. If our brains aren't made for this hyper-connected era, it makes sense that the habits most likely to benefit our mental health are ancient.

Regardless of what we're thinking, our brain is working hard. It's composed of approximately 100 billion neurons (equivalent to the number of stars in the Milky Way), that carry information travelling up to 430 kilometres (270 miles) per hour. The brain uses 20 per cent of all the energy (oxygen and calories) our body requires each day, despite it only weighing 2 kilograms (4½ pounds).

Our minds are naturally cluttered with repetitive thoughts and ruminations. It's a little like the flow of your house: you walk the same route from one room to another and back again as you go about your day. This is how you live in your home. How you live in your brain is very similar: the same thoughts and patterns create well-worn pathways that are tricky to step off. We have to intentionally set out on a different pathway – walk it again and again and again – to establish some level of comfort so it becomes habitual. This is a habit shift. It's also a very basic explanation of neuroplasticity – the brain's ability to reorganise and form neural connections if we repeat new thoughts and behaviours.

This is how you can create breathing space for yourself – consider it a habit, practise it consistently, create a new neural pathway.

HOW WE FORM HABITS

It's commonly thought that the mind dictates habits, but it's actually your environment that has the most control. Because we're making so many tiny decisions each day, the brain creates habits to automate our behaviour. But as Dr Gina Cleo, who is at the forefront of habit research, says, all habits need a trigger, and often that is our environment.

Habits are established through repetition; we have to do something again and again and again to form a habit. But what exactly is happening in the brain to ensure this new routine becomes habitual? A new neural pathway is created, so if you continue practising this new habit – writing first thing in the morning, going for a jog at 6 am, lying down to do 10 minutes of deep breathing at 2.30 pm – the nerves forming that neural pathway are gradually covered with extra layers of something called a myelin sheath, which makes it stronger and more established. It's like the pathway is sealed, and less likely to be washed away in the next storm.

No matter how chaotic and messy, unscripted and surprising your day is, these habits can offer you stability; you can lean on them however discombobulated you feel. Of course, you need to see value in them, so a quick reminder of the steps involved:

1. *Understand what your brain needs to be creative and productive.*
2. *Figure out what rest looks like for you.*
3. *Integrate that rest into your normal.*
4. *Continue practising so it becomes habitual – so it's something you do, not something you necessarily need to think about.*

Thoughts are habitual (you have most of the same thoughts today as you had yesterday) and subjective (they're exclusive to you, based on your unique perspective on the world). Your experience of life is generated from your thoughts – from the inside out – but most people believe it's the other way around, that the outside dictates what you feel. Your entire experience of life – emotions and reactions – is created from within you via thought. A quote often attributed to Anaïs Nin says it beautifully: 'We don't see things as they are; we see them as we are.' Thoughts become feelings, which influence mood and, when repeated over months, become our temperament. When these repetitions continue over years, we develop personality traits.

Thoughts are much like breath: if you don't hold your breath, a new one rushes in without your control. And if you don't hold your thoughts, identify them and attach to them, they will arrive and leave without your control. Both breath and thought flow.

How does this flow influence our habits? Well, our brain does better in certain, predictable situations. Uncertainty unravels us. That's why establishing a routine is encouraged if you feel like you're flailing.

What we know about habits is that they can become a strong structure for us to lean on. Essentially, they give us a really good reason to focus our attention. They're bidirectional: when you create a new habit, you break an old one. It's just as effective to place emphasis on the new habit you're nurturing as it is to consciously let go of the old habit you're eradicating. When we change our habits, we change our subconscious behaviour. These new habits become automatic – they're instinctive, we do them without even thinking about it, which means they're not contributing to our mental load, they're actually relieving it.

Dr Cleo explains that habits are more than just simple behaviours – they say a lot about who we are. If, like me, you recoil at early January's catchcry, *New year, new you!* because the thought of making change for a whole year feels too big to contemplate, you'll be comforted to know that science agrees. In fact, if you want to make a long-term change, the only proven method is to focus on one day at a time, starting with today. As Cleo explains in her book *The Habit Revolution*, 'making consistent, achievable, bite-sized changes in our day-to-day life to alter our habits is the only scientifically backed system for achieving sustainable success'.

Breaking our scrolling habit

If we consider what is preventing us from accessing breathing space – or is actually taking up the space – most of us would agree that our phones come to mind. Why are we so addicted? Because we naturally seek rewards and avoid pain, and scrolling on socials is a form of self-indulgence. One of the reasons we scroll on our phone is that it provides pleasure-producing stimuli that are much more enjoyable than whatever we're bored by or procrastinating on. Dopamine is addictive and we become tolerant to it, so we want more than we did yesterday. We then fall into a dopamine-deficient state, which can lead us into anxiety, depression and insomnia, and exacerbate a sense of hopelessness. It's a dismal reality, but sometimes knowing the facts can be just what we need to consciously do something about it.

US psychiatrist Dr Anna Lembke refers to social media as a 'digital drug' – our phones are turning us into 'digital junkies'. It's abrasive language, but the poisonous effect of social media on the creative mind – its seeping of trust and courage and, sometimes, self-worth – is exactly what we need to be honest about if we're going to make conscious, lasting, consistent change. Numbers can help, too. Artist and writer August Lamm has dug deeper than the surface 'phones are bad' discourse to offer statistics that are impossible to deny: if you spend three hours a day on your phone, it equates to 10 years of your adult life. It was one question they asked that shook me: 'Is this how you want to spend your life? This is how you are spending your life.'

I see it in myself and so many people: the longing for breathing room but the reality of a busy life. It's really hard to create that space because all the systems that infiltrate our lives are designed to be addictive. So even if you don't want to be scrolling or checking your notifications, you do it, while the voice inside your head says: *Stop, you need to go outside.*

But as one study of people who reported high levels of stress shows, 12 per cent said that feeling like they needed to respond to messages instantly was a stressor. We live in a world where immediacy is championed, so we have to take really considered steps not to exist in a perpetual state of urgency. Scrolling social media can leave us anxious, with a vague sense of unease, feeding a panic that we're not *doing enough*. If we're always switched on, our brain is gobbling up as much information as it possibly can, alert to and delighted by the pings and beeps.

Cleo believes that if we want to be less distracted by our phones we need to practise self-binding. 'I have no-phone times in my day and no-phone zones in my house. I choose not to have it around me. A lot of the time we try to use self-control or willpower, which are fleeting resources. We need to create a supportive environment rather than relying on grit and tenacity.'

Consider your phone an efficiency tool

Of course our phones make life easier. But when we pay attention to the way they enhance and detract from everyday life, we can utilise their benefits without losing hours mindlessly scrolling. Is this easy? No. After all, you are essentially retraining your brain and catching yourself in moments of instinctive distraction. This requires constant awareness. But do it one day and then another, and slowly but surely you're creating a new, healthier habit.

It's a bit like an early morning run – you may hate it at first, but you'll be so glad you did it once you're home, drinking a big glass of water and enjoying the endorphin rush. If you want agency over your time, it starts with your phone. Can you hone the ability to pick it up, complete the task – transfer money, reply to a message, check the tides – and then promptly put it down again? Perhaps this is something you can practise this week. And it does take practice – but be encouraged by the fact that every time you do it, you're reinforcing a new habit that will eventually become instinctive.

The design of our brain sucks us in

We naturally have a scarcity mindset that means the most primal part of our brain thinks: *I'd better get this now, because it might not be there later.* Avik Basu points to the fact that seeking and consuming information is actually instinctive; we're not even thinking about what we're doing – we're hungry for information so we gulp it till we're bursting. We're glued to our phones because they make this process easy.

Basu likens it to stumbling upon an abundance of fruit in ancestral times; the most primal thing to do would be to eat it all because food was scarce and you never knew when the next meal would come. Your body would then store the extra fat, which would serve you in leaner times. We need to think about information the same way.

'You're eating up all the useful, intriguing information all the time,' Basu says. 'Our brains are designed to receive that information in infrequent amounts and now it's 24/7, whenever you want it, open your phone and find something interesting. It's not being stored as fat but mental clutter, and competing with other purposes and intentions we have. This isn't even a mindset, think of it as more about instinct: we're not even thinking about it, we're instinctively consuming the information.'

In an attention economy Basu likens our information overload to shopping in a homewares store: it's easy to keep buying and hoarding objects till your house is cluttered. 'The mind is like that too,' he says. 'We are being sold information that's exciting and interesting, and our brains are designed to pick up on those things. It just so happens that the informational environment we live in has been engineered to capture our attention, adding more clutter to an already cluttered space, so we need tools to let go of some clutter, to let it fade away.'

A yearly subscription to an app blocker is both consocious consumerism and a really practical step towards creating a supportive environment. It's a self-imposed boundary that, in turn, creates breathing space.

The *Oxford English Dictionary*'s 2024 'word' of the year was 'brain rot', and while psychologists say that consuming digital content is not having the literal effects that the phrase conjures, I think we can all agree that in a time where disillusion is rife and we're divided as a result, it may be beneficial to start looking out instead of down at the black screen in our palm. Our collective malaise is in part due to our lack of attention. Studies show that on average, we spend a mere 40 seconds viewing something on a screen before we skip on to the next thing in line.

Space is right here

We've come to equate breathing space with a holiday, but space in the mind shouldn't be as transient as a holiday. And you shouldn't have to leave your home – and your life – to take a breather. Essential habits aren't dependent on grand gestures, and they're not something you chase out there. They're actually right here, right where you are. Novelist and playwright Saul Bellow calls this 'stillness in the midst of chaos'. He was referring to art, but art and life are much the same. Any mother corralling children through the day and night knows the seeking of stillness in her bones, as do parents sandwiched in midlife or professionals juggling a persistently stressful career. Bellow thinks it has something to do with 'an arrest of attention in the midst of distraction'. 'Arrest' may be abrasive, but in a distracted world, it's necessary.

Research shows that mindful breathing – which is considered a form of meditation – increases a positive perspective and results in higher levels of

optimism, significantly impacting negativity bias. If
we are innately pessimistic creatures, and we know
the weight of negative emotions – the heaviness
of grief, the cloud of anger – it makes sense that
these feelings oppress tiny instants of joy, both in
the moment and in our memories. Intentional times
throughout the day, when we turn our attention to
our breath, lengthening and softening our inhalation
and exhalation, can help us create space in the mind,
allowing a more positive outlook. It's a pernicious
myth that we should be aiming for happiness in life,
but it's good for us to move through our days with
a more positive slant.

THE MYTH OF MULTITASKING

Multitasking is celebrated, particularly for women, who are
conditioned to think it's a sign that they're doing things right
and they're doing them well. But it's actually a non-existent
cognitive skill – the human brain is incapable of doing it.

We're single-minded creatures – our brain can only produce
one to two thoughts in the conscious mind at once, which is
why the common habit of switching between tasks and screens
is so detrimental. It even has a name: 'the switch cost effect' –
your distraction is costing you time, as is the refocus required
when you return to your original task.

Of course you can try and do more than one thing at a time,
but it's actually an inefficient way of doing things – we're
slower and less attentive when we live and work this way.
Knowing this helps us understand why those of us required
to blend caregiving with paid employment and staying on
top of the washing pile find it almost impossible to carve

out downtime. Mothers are culturally expected to know exactly how to care for their babies as soon as they're born, and societally expected to return to who they were before pregnancy – and to do it with ease and joy. Read: be the ultimate multitaskers, because the world benefits immensely when we strive to do it all and we strive to do it well. This is reflected in the statistic that the unpaid care industry is worth $650 billion annually (equivalent to three mining sectors).

Understanding what your brain is capable of – how it works and thrives – is moving one step closer to creating space in your mind. And yet multitasking is how most of us move through the day, because our diaries are full and we're accustomed to moving quickly. We gorge on what we see and hear, stop what we're doing to respond immediately to emails and phone calls; we skim-read messages and dart from one meeting or appointment to the next. And all the trails of information we're digesting are stored for later while our brain stays alert and vigilant. The brain is a primal organ; its job is to keep you alive. But left to its own devices, it focuses on fear (this is our innate negativity bias). This is why creativity, handiwork and goal-setting are vital for our sense of contentment and joy. Instead of darting between tasks and staying alert to threat, our brain is stimulated and fulfilled by the process of making and progressing – one focused thing at a time.

How to do one thing at a time

Remember when Dr Cleo said that one element of phone control was to create a supportive environment? The same goes for doing one thing at a time. Start small – set an alarm for 10 minutes and clear the kitchen bench (always a magnet for clutter). If you're at your desk, the Pomodoro method is helpful to keep you on track: you work for 25 minutes and then step away from your desk for a five-minute break. After four rounds you take a longer break of 15–30 minutes. It's a helpful boundary that's particularly useful when we feel overwhelmed or stressed, which is when we procrastinate easily.

As with all habits, if we practise it regularly, we're training our brain – creating new neural pathways, and improving our attention span and ability to focus. Everywhere I look, people are discussing attention, the fact that the technology that made life easier has also robbed us of the ability to focus and go deep – think, create, read, write, converse. Meaningful memories are created in meaningful moments. Intentionally create them and savour them – you have agency over this!

FIVE WAYS TO ...
Check your habits

1. Track your spending. Unconscious spending is the norm, but the first step to establishing some semblance of control over your money (and your time) is to track each dollar so you understand your spending habits.

2. Look at your phone usage. Yes, it's confronting, but it's also evidence of how much time you could have to do things that are meaningful to you (and good for your brain). Remember that establishing a new habit also helps you break the old.

3. Ask yourself if you're trying to keep up with impossible standards. If you find yourself in a berating cycle of wanting to improve, it may be helpful to ask yourself what you're aiming for.

4. Figure out what your priorities are. What matters to you each day? How do you want to feel? These are big questions, but keep asking them: the answers will guide your decision-making.

5. Schedule rest and joy. This means you're taking care of yourself and you're prioritising the experiences that nourish and bolster you. Normal life may involve some really hard, unavoidable stuff, but that doesn't mean you can't intentionally lighten the load with soothing, grounding habits.

7

Savour the good

We have an innate negativity bias, but our wellness and survival depend on a balance of optimism and pessimism. That's why we need to savour our positive experiences.

Negative experiences – fears, feelings and encounters – have a greater impact on our psychological state than positive ones. The memories we form through these experiences are stronger and more vivid than the positive. They also last longer. A simplistic picture of our brain's catalogue of memories would lean towards a collection of stories where we felt hurt, humiliation, resentment and jealousy – dark, sad, uncomfortable stories, when bad decisions were made and harsh words were spoken. We have an innate negativity bias. This helps us understand why it is vital to revel in moments of joy – holding ourselves in the experience so we can be enveloped in the *feeling* of it and think: *Remember how this feels*. It extends the joy and allows the brain to map these moments and file them away as precious stories worth keeping. This is the essence of ancient rites and rituals, revered markers of time that acknowledge and celebrate the milestones: coming of age, the turning of seasons, love and unity, new life; and also the ordinary yet remarkable daily happenings: sun and rain, connection with people we love, making with our hands, sharing a meal.

It's important to understand this about your brain if you want to live with more contentment and creativity. Negativity prevents us from trying new things – creating and making – which are practices that allow us to feel happiness in the moment. New research also suggests that seeking out new experiences and reflecting on positive ones is how we can slow down our perception of time. 'Find the time and space to do the things that you're going to remember,' suggests Dr Ruth Ogden from Liverpool John Moores University in a *Guardian* article. 'And spend time reminiscing about good things that have happened to you. Because the more we keep these memories alive, the more we're likely to feel like the year was longer.' Dr Marc Wittmann from the Institute for Frontier Areas of Psychology and Mental Health in Germany calls this subjective experience 'felt time'. It's the opposite of objective 'clock time'.

It's also backed by the concept of scarcity: if we have too little of something – commonly time and money – our mind focuses on the lack of it and we're left feeling (and believing) that we don't have enough. We then adopt tunnel vision, which inhibits decision-making and creative solutions. It's a phenomenon well documented in psychology: if the mind is focused on one thing, other abilities and skills – attention, self-control and long-term planning – often suffer. Behavioural economist Dr Sendhil Mullainathan and psychologist Dr Eldar Shafir conducted research on scarcity's most insidious effects, including a mindset that rarely considers our long-term best interests. This nods to our contemporary understanding of a busy life and our perceived lack of time.

We're not resting in the breathing space because we don't believe it even exists.

BE AWARE OF YOUR ATTITUDE TO TIME

In the richest countries in the world, we have more leisure time than we've ever had and we don't necessarily know what to do with it. It makes us uncomfortable and so we distract ourselves. Dr Anna Lembke refers to this as the 'plenty paradox' – we've surpassed abundance and it's changing our brains and leading us into a dopamine-deficient state. Lembke refers to time in light of our 'diffuse addiction to the internet' – are we really that busy, or are we moving so quickly that we're surpassing the free time that exists?

On the flipside, the more we're cemented in routine and experiencing boredom in our everyday life, the faster time passes in retrospect. It's why time speeds up for adults – who have long-established routines – and why childhood seemingly stretches out: it's brimming with new experiences every day. But this isn't to say you have to have constant new experiences to savour time. Studies show that simply being attentive to life and noticing the new details is one way of processing fresh information and, in turn, slowing the hours. Of course, the habit most likely to speed up time and make us feel like we've wasted it is social media. The research is not yet published, but the results aren't surprising. We all know what it feels like to look up from the screen and be aghast at the time that has passed.

Our attitude to time regulates our days. We bemoan the loss of it, feel disenchanted by the racing hours. As life gets quicker, we find ourselves grasping for time. Our obligations dictate our schedules, we fear wasting it, we aim to make the most of it. And that's because a country's economic wellbeing is the single largest determinant for the pace of life. The wealthier we are, the faster we move, the more we watch the clock. If you live like this, every hour holds potential and, therefore, every hour not used is wasted. And yet human perception of time is subjective: it slows down or speeds up depending on what we're doing. It's 'felt time'. And so what if we started thinking that life is actually long? What if we actually have plenty of time to do the things that we want and need to do, but instead we're trapped in the mindset that we need to hurry because the hours are disintegrating?

When we're rushing, we're skipping past all the good stuff – we're so caught up in all the things we need to do that we don't even notice the time that exists all around us. If you're living in a way that doesn't align with your values, perhaps it does feel like life is short; maybe this is the realisation you need to make change.

Rubber time

In Indonesia there's a phrase – jam karet – that translates to 'rubber time'. It's a nod to the flexibility and uncertainty of time that expands and shrinks like rubber. If you've ever visited Bali, you'll experience this mentality, which is embedded in the culture. There is never a sense of urgency on the Island of the Gods, but instead a relaxed ease imbued with the inherent slowness that humidity dictates. No one is concerned with the accuracy of time but instead considers the quality of it in relation to the people they're with. 'Where does the time go?' we say. 'Time is racing.' And in Bali they say, 'Tidak apa-apa' (It doesn't matter). Is this because they live in a world not of time but of space, a commodity that cannot be measured, that's both infinite and only of the now?

SAVOUR THE JOY

Positive feelings don't linger like the negative; authors recall the bad reviews easily, whereas the glowing endorsements fade into the background. Insults become ingrained whereas praise is fleeting. Negative triggers influence our habits more than positive ones, and we naturally ruminate over negative experiences but don't invest nearly as much thought or analysis in the positive. Research shows that this negativity bias is present from birth; infants pay closest attention to what they don't like.

Our biological and psychological response to negative events is hardwired; fear of danger keeps us out of harm's way. This innate pessimism has a purpose; it's a survival mechanism. If we were always chasing and looking for the good, we wouldn't be as vigilant and therefore protected from danger. We wouldn't be paying attention. This hypervigilance from perceived threat is how we exist – even if the threats are not as imminent as a lion creeping towards us on a sparse plain – and I can't help but think that this is why we naturally skim over the joy in life. This is why we need to bring all of our attention to the moments that spark within us delight and rapture – however fleeting – to ensure we don't live a life of drudgery. That way the happiness lightens the load a little, allows us to move with more energy and verve.

Savouring doesn't come naturally though; it has to be intentional. Consider it a skill to cultivate as a step towards creating a happier mindset. It's a habit that can help restore your attention so you're more likely to notice the good that already exists in your days (and in your life). If you've ever kept a gratitude journal, you've savoured past experiences by reflecting and reminiscing to continue enjoying them through memory. This is one part of the Savoring Beliefs Inventory, a measure created by psychologist Dr Fred Bryant. The other two pillars include practising 'a degree of conscious enjoyment' in the present and 'keenly anticipating' what's to come.

We saw earlier that our body inherits its stress and trauma response from our ancestors to ensure our survival. In a similar way, while our brain cells store and assemble memories, new research shows that cells in the body can learn and form memories too. And so trauma and stress will imprint on us, acting as a cellular protective mechanism. If our bodies and brains are therefore innately pessimistic, it makes sense that we need to consciously create breathing space to ensure we have reprieve in the form of feel-good chemicals that move through us, igniting a deep sense of wonder. Sometimes we have to create the joy for ourselves, sometimes we have to chase it. But even the sense of anticipation is worthwhile (look to any child counting down the days to a birthday party, and the giddiness is palpable).

Our survival and wellness require a balance of optimism and pessimism, distinct modes of thinking that exist on a continuum. Too optimistic and we become reckless, too pessimistic and life is miserable.

To do this we need to be aware and attentive, two skills that we're losing in an age of hyper-convenience. In a distracted world of quick-fire content, awareness and attention take work – focusing very intentionally on what you're doing now, in this very moment. If you feel like you've lost your ability to concentrate, understanding how to restore your attention is the first step. And then? Become aware of what psychologists call 'reward sensitivity' – essentially the drive to seek and experience happiness. This is dependent on noticing and savouring positive emotions, and it's often emphasised in cognitive therapy – enhance positive experiences to boost your joy rather than focusing on the eradication of emotions that cause discomfort and pain. It begins, as all new habits do, with intention.

Little treats are small joys

Just as we need to balance optimism and pessimism for wellness, we need to find an even keel between sensibleness and indulgence. We all love a small treat, and yet it's evolved to become an umbrella term for everything from a pastry with our coffee to a weekend in a fancy hotel on a whim. Journalist Imogen West-Knights refers to it as 'treat brain' in her 2021 article for the *Financial Times*, saying it is a consequence of pandemic lockdowns and our need to soothe ourselves when we lost all of our certainties.

Indeed, that's why we reach for all comforts: for stability when life is uncertain. But small joys aren't always things you buy. I don't think we need to give up treats altogether – life just isn't that rigid – and I think there is always good reason to buy a new book and read it while sipping a coffee from your favourite cafe (or whatever your small, joyful ideal is). But I think it can also be helpful to find joy in simplicity and sufficiency: using what you've got, mending something that's broken, learning a new skill, joining a book club, going on a long walk in the middle of the week and leaving all the to-dos behind. These things ignite a sense of wonder in the little parcel of the world we call home and, with time, they prompt us to become more critical thinkers and conscious consumers.

Share the good moments

One way to seek and savour joyful moments is to share them. Small acts of care are an acknowledgement of what someone else needs, but a happy offering also yields inspiration and contentment, especially when it's unexpected.

A meal on a doorstep, a message to check in, a congratulations cake, an offer to help, a book because it may help, an invitation to join, hand-me-downs because they no longer fit, a donation to pay it forward, a look in the eye that says: 'I see you and I think you're wonderful.'

FIVE WAYS TO ...
Savour the good

1. Take note of remarkable ordinary things. These are the simple things in life that instil a sense of contentment and bolster us. They remind us of what really matters: a beautiful cup warmed by the tea it holds, a flickering beeswax candle, a bird's nest uncovered once the leaves have fallen in autumn, a movie that makes you cry, a new leaf on your indoor plant, a clear winter sky.

2. Walk with the intention to observe. When you pay attention to your surroundings you're more likely to notice the beauty you often bypass. Look past the stains and urban mishaps and train your eyes to see the good.

3. Share your positive experiences with others. Research shows that when we do this, we're essentially capitalising on the good. This, in turn, bolsters social connection, which increases positive mood and overall wellbeing.

4. Eat slowly. When we chew mindfully and eat when we're at ease, our digestion improves. And when we eat comfort food? Our body releases oxytocin, the hormone that relaxes and heals and makes us feel good.

5. Cultivate contentment for the home you have, its functionality and comfort, even if it doesn't look like anything you see on socials. Most of us live in normal homes that keep us warm and protected, even if we have a messy laundry, mismatched chairs, fingerprints on the walls and chipped paint on the eaves.

Restore your attention

In our distracted lives, we need to make a conscious choice to pay attention. But to do this we first require an understanding of our brain's resources.

In everyday life, we're accumulating mental garbage – concepts, ideas, images, hundreds of tiny thought threads – that collect and compete for our attention. This general busyness puts a significant burden on the prefrontal cortex of the brain, the region involved in higher-order thinking (such as critical thinking and problem-solving). These small demands accumulate to drain our attentional resources and the result is distraction and cognitive fatigue (*I can't think straight, I can't possibly answer a question or make a decision right now.*)

We understand what it means to declutter our home: sorting all the miscellany that gathers, keeping what we need, letting go of what we don't. A similar process needs to occur to create space in our mind – sorting the keepsakes from the not-needed. This clearing of space is vital for living and thinking well, for reducing stress and having the capacity to create, answer big questions and find solutions. This is difficult in a world engineered to hold our attention on a screen, and yet in the scope of humanity, it's a normal, everyday occurrence and it happened in all the leisure time that existed between hunting and gathering.

The process isn't complicated, either. The simple yet increasingly rare practice of reflection is actually incredibly accessible. This gives the prefrontal cortex time to rest, and this stillness of mind allows insights and solutions to bubble up to the surface from the subconscious to the conscious in a way that's constructive and helpful.

RESTORING YOUR ATTENTION

Reflection isn't happenstance for most of us; it's something we need to be intentional with. And it's not always easy, because in modern life there is deep discomfort in waiting. It's essentially another endangered ancient habit, because it just isn't necessary in so many aspects of our lives where most things are convenient and immediate. It also feels and often looks like nothing – staring into the distance, letting your attention and your gaze gently move from one thing to the next, sitting still. It can feel aimless and it's therefore hard to attach meaning to it. But as environmental psychologist Avik Basu explains, it's one of the most practical ways to restore our attention.

Attention is what allows us to focus on what's relevant and tune out what's not. One of the major tenets of attention restoration theory (ART) is that humans have two types of attention:

1. **directed attention**, *a finite resource directed by
    our thinking brain that is controlling what we
    pay attention to. After a long day of work, you'll
    likely find it hard to concentrate because you've
    exhausted your directed attention.*
2. **effortless or involuntary attention**, *which is
    captured by intriguing but not arresting stimuli.
    Compare the way you look around you as you walk
    down the street with the way you engage with
    a screen.*

When you reach the point in your day when you can't
possibly make one more decision and you can't focus on what
you're doing, you're experiencing directed-attention fatigue
(DAF). But what most of us do when we feel the discomfort
and frustration of this experience is push through despite
waning cognitive ability – or scroll. This form of distraction is
the opposing force to space and rest. When you're distracted,
you're pulled away from yourself. If you feel like the days
are passing too quickly – a blip and they're gone – you're
likely distracted. Don't feel bad about this, it's most of us –
entrenched in routine with a phone not far away at
all times.

One way of restoring our attention is through finding
breathing space. There have been countless studies on the
benefits of nature for our physiology and psychology, as
Dr Lara Bertolino explains: 'We know from literature that
having an experience of awe can be really healing. It can help
people with perspective. There are big, common lessons we
can learn from nature. Diversity of ecosystems, cycles of light
and dark, reciprocity, biodiversity – they're potent, high-level
messages and they can help us make sense of ourselves.'

The fact that many people live without access to nature –
usually those in urban environments where green and blue
spaces haven't been a planning priority – has consequences.
Basu believes the price of living in modern environments
is reflected in the rates of overwork, stress and burnout.
'This is the cost we're paying for living in a vastly different
environment to the one our brains evolved in,' he says. And
yet we can intentionally seek out non-taxing spaces even if we
can't go for a walk in a forest. Washing the dishes, watering
the garden, folding washing and showering allow the thinking
brain to take a backseat.

*Breathing space exists in the waiting time: the coffee
line, school pick-up lane, doctor's surgery, the minutes
before a friend arrives. Observe what's happening
around you, bring your awareness to your breath, jot
some thoughts on paper, soften your body.*

Attention restoration theory

The concept of attention restoration theory (ART) was
formulated in the 1980s by Rachel and Stephen Kaplan,
professors at the University of Michigan who specialised in
environmental psychology, specifically the benefits of nature.
Natural stimulation is softly fascinating: it captures our
attention but not all of our attentional resources, which means
our mind can still wander. In nature, our prefrontal cortex isn't
active, which gives our brain's default network (also known
as the imagination network) space to play. This is when our
mind wanders and our subconscious pushes memories, ideas
and interesting thoughts to the surface. Even the words 'soft
fascination' evoke a sense of calm and ease. On the flipside,

'hard fascination' is anything that's difficult to turn away from – sirens in the street, a gratuitous movie, social media that's designed to hold our attention.

When we can't employ our attention it can make us feel irritable and impatient because we can't think clearly – everything feels muddled. The solution is time in nature. The key to switching off the thinking part of our brain to make space for our imagination is access to a mellow, low-energy environment where our attention is gently captured. No one is exhausted from looking at a waterfall or the branches of a tree swaying with the wind. We can zone out while we're looking at them, and when we do this, we stop clawing at the endless thoughts we have and let our brain do the good work of sorting and making space.

The process of restoring attention

As we've seen, when our directed attention wanes, DAF sets in. However, if we interrupt DAF with effortless attention, we skip the fatigue and the subsequent backtracking it requires.

1. **Directed attention (concentration)**: This is the starting point, where directed attention is available and it's possible to concentrate on tasks.
2. **Directed attention fatigue**: As our directed attention is exhausted, fatigue sets in. We find it increasingly difficult to focus, and distractions become more appealing.
3. **Effortless attention (soft fascination)**: When we engage in activities that don't require directed attention or we spend time in

restorative environments (such as nature),
our brain enters a state of effortless attention.
This period of soft fascination allows for
reflection and starts to replenish our depleted
attention resources, eventually restoring our
directed attention.

Soft fascination

'What we have found is that by being in natural environments –
ones that are resonating with our evolutionary past – they
invoke a state of soft fascination in us,' Basu says. 'Your
attention is captured softly, it's not arrested like it is by social
media – that is, information engineered to completely capture
your attention and not make you want to turn away. Nature
isn't quite like that; nature allows plenty of turning away and
that then allows the resolution of internal threads that keep
accumulating in the mind.'

I casually refer to soft fascination as 'awe's little sister'.
There's been a lot of talk about awe in recent years thanks to
the science that proves how beneficial it is for our wellbeing: it
bolsters our connection with the natural world, it's delightfully
'measured in goosebumps', and it pulls us out of our own
mental misery and reminds us that our small problems are
inconsequential in the grand scheme of things. But when we set
out to find something awe-inspiring, we quickly learn that you
can't force goosebumps. And sometimes when we're looking for
the unforgettable, we skip over the ordinary beauty that exists
right in front of us.

Lightly focusing our awareness on everyday things – the
steam rising from a cup of tea; the pattern of tiles on the
bathroom wall; sheets billowing on the line; the embedded

optimism of seedlings pushing up towards the light; the quiet, subtle parts of your day that pique your attention but don't wholly occupy your mind – is commonly referred to as 'mindfulness without the meditation'. It can be filed in the same category as shinrin-yoku (forest bathing; see page 238) because it has significant physiological and cognitive benefits.

'A little slice of soft fascination is what our ancestors would have experienced quite often and very regularly,' Basu says. 'Now we have to seek it out and we have to make sure society has spaces that are available, in order to restore this scarce resource.' He explains that regardless of our mental state – whether we're confused or bored or feeling tired – seeking out soft fascination is always worthwhile. 'Soft fascination is not necessarily tied to any one thing – you can be in a state of confusion and benefit from soft fascination because it clears out some clutter and helps you find clarity,' he says. 'If you're bored and you're in nature, that would give you enough time and space to allow you to become curious about something and that naturally leads you down a path of creative thought.'

When we clear space, we allow our imagination network to come to the forefront of our mind – it's no longer clouded by excess information. And if we exist in the space that's been created instead of being lured by distraction, we will eventually reach the point of curiosity. Instead of hard, focused attention, we engage in what is referred to as 'light focus'. This isn't a skill we need to learn – we already do this throughout our week – but just knowing this practice has a name can be rather enlightening. I find it especially comforting as a creative person. I *know* the mental reprieve of letting my mind wander. Allowing my focus to settle on ordinary things bolsters my thinking brain. Having language to define it? Well, it's almost like I have a deeper understanding of myself – how I tick, think, reflect and create. This is so incredibly encouraging.

It's not woo-woo either, it's science! Psychologists have even researched exactly how much time we need to spend softly fascinated for it to be beneficial. Studies show that when we're in a green space we're lightly focusing on what's around us. But there's a catch: we only benefit if our phone is switched off or, better yet, not with us at all. In a time-poor culture that grasps for spare minutes, there's also a helpful set timeframe to reap the rewards: 20 minutes, ideally three times a week, lowers our cortisol levels. The cognitive effects? A calmer, sharper mind that's more creative and productive.

Soft fascination is like downtime for our brain, which is why it's such a powerful practice for everyone, but especially those who are engaged in hours of directed attention on a regular basis. Nature allows us to move through it with a lightness of being, which creates space for self-reflection and mental reprieve. The results? Mental decluttering, clearer thoughts, more aha moments.

Even mundane, everyday tasks have a restorative potential. It's why we have lightbulb moments in the shower, or can figure out the solution to problems while we walk or hang out the washing. Sometimes it's lying on the bed, staring at the ceiling and just allowing ourselves to be in the nothingness. In a noisy, bright world that constantly demands our attention, soft fascination is mental breathing space.

Soft fascination is mental cushioning for a life that's increasingly demanding. It feels like a tangible way to create a more sustainable, creative life. Go slow to go far. Restore your attention to sharpen your mind.

*Regardless of when you do it and why you're doing it,
it's always beneficial.*

Avik Basu explains this typical thought pattern, which isn't
necessarily linear but cycles back and forth:

confusion – clarity – boredom – curiosity

'When you're learning something, you go through a process.
Let's say you're in the middle of it and you're confused – it's
uncomfortable and a bit painful. And then you come to a place
of clarity – your aha moment. Now all the confusion doesn't
plague you, you feel good (even though it doesn't last very
long) and after that comes boredom because you don't have the
problem to work on any more. This is a sign that there's space
for something new to come in.'

It's at this moment that we distract ourselves by picking
up our phone, because boredom, like confusion, and perhaps
even pain, doesn't feel good. But this distraction – hard
fascination – doesn't allow space for an idea to spark,
and so we forgo the path of curiosity and creativity for
mindless consumption.

'We have an easy fix for boredom now, whereas in the 1990s
we didn't, but boredom serves a function,' Basu says. 'It's saying,
"Fill my brain with more stuff. I'm looking for something."
From that boredom comes curiosity, because the brain is always
looking.' The word boredom has its roots in the old English
beran, meaning to carry, endure, give birth to. Boredom is
the (often uncomfortable) waiting before seeds of new ideas
are planted. That's how we can attach meaning to it; it's the
necessary space required before the bright thinking.

Soft fascination is a form of breathing space and it's available to us all, regardless of where and how we live. The answer lies in individual small experiments. You have to see what works for you. And, as Basu says, the cost of doing it is relatively low – it doesn't impinge on your time or financial resources.

'You could tend to a house plant, look at a tree out the window, but where the challenge is, and I think this is more and more true, comes back to the alternatives for your attention,' he says. 'Attention is a human function that's designed to have us attend to things that will save us, help us avoid danger and plan for the future. The problem is that soft fascination, as charming as it is, is competing against things that are engineered. The charming doesn't win out against the addictive.'

But it can, if we choose to romanticise and savour it, to put the phone away and let our gaze wander instead. When we intentionally let our brain breathe, we begin to form a foundation for happiness, health and creativity.

GET CURIOUS AND CATEGORISE

If you have ever spent time outside with small children, you will know their penchant for collecting things: rocks, sticks, shells, feathers. Of course, to small hands and an inquisitive mind, these precious finds are worth pocketing for the simple fact that they feel like treasure. When these pieces of nature come into the home and line the windowsill, it is an act of documentation and ornamentation. But what children are doing is categorising, literally creating order and coherence in their world. They do it with colour-coded blocks, cars and trucks and little wooden animals, too. It's not a process relegated to childhood, either. If you've reached your thirties and become particularly charmed by birdwatching or vegetable gardening, or you feel comforted by your daily habits, this is because patterns in our life and in nature feel meaningful to us; they seem reliable and often steadfast. A scientist looks for patterns to support a hypothesis; writers are guided by patterns to get to the truth of their words – all of us understand who we are and where we belong when we are attentive to the patterns of our life.

Categorisation helps us simplify and organise our complex world, which allows us to respond to new experiences efficiently. Essentially, being able to categorise allows us to control the controllable. It helps us nurture a sense of predictability (which our brain loves) and allows us to make sense of things that help us find meaning.

The power of handiwork

When we use our hands on a task that doesn't demand much of us cognitively, our brain can effectively switch off from concentration mode and wander. Modern life is increasingly sedentary – so many tasks we once did with our hands now require the press of a button – and yet we were designed to use our hands and bodies to stay active and engaged with life. Our brain is hardwired for meaningful action. This ensured we left the comfortable cave we slept in to hunt food and gather firewood so we stayed alive.

When you're engaging in the ancient habit of doing things with your hands – washing dishes, gardening, kneading dough, drawing, knitting, threading beads, sewing on a button, weaving, wringing a cloth and wiping a dusty shelf – the 'effort-driven reward circuit' in your brain is ignited. This is because the action and effort of using your hands produces a result. It's purposeful, meaningful work – your progress is tangible and visible, and that's rewarding. Convenience essentially deprives the brain of these rewards.

CLOSE THE MENTAL TABS BY GETTING THINGS DONE

Productivity isn't a bad thing. Things need to be done in life – often obligatory tasks that aren't much fun. And while our brain does better if we have consistent periods of rest, there's no getting around the fact that sometimes we just need to do whatever is pressing.

But I've got so much to do, my list is never done! you may moan. And that's when I would encourage you to set aside an hour every week, or a whole morning, maybe even a day, to do the things that are bugging you with their nagging persistence. Call it purposefully productive, or clearing the slate, or ticking off the necessary to-dos. Maybe it deserves the title of Life Admin Day. If all the jobs you don't want to do have accumulated to the point that they're a constant presence in your mind, preventing you from accessing any space, then perhaps you need to deal with them first.

So let's start in the best way we know how – a list. A nice pen helps, perhaps even a colourful set of highlighters. But you could also use your notes app or the back of your electricity bill. Use what you've got, start right where you are. What needs to be done? Most likely an appointment booked, a return slip printed, the bank called. Perhaps you need to locate a missing library book, complete a funding questionnaire, answer a long email or pick up an online grocery order. I bet your quarterly tax needs doing and collating receipts feels like one task too many …

As you jot down each item, really ask yourself if it's truly urgent or if it will be only a small inconvenience if you don't get it done. If, like me, you easily catastrophise, this is a practical way of sifting through the list and being really honest about the true importance of your undone tasks.

So make yourself a cup of something nice and dedicate your time getting through the list of things you've been putting off. This is what this day is for. With each task done, you'll build momentum, and within a few hours you'll be delighting in the satisfaction of ticking items off your list and clearing the slate.

And perhaps at the bottom of that list, when the ticks have accumulated like celebratory flags down the side of the page, you can add a little treat. I know there's a lot of criticism of 'treat culture', but it's simply a response to the capitalist world we live in. If millennials can't afford houses, they should be able to treat themselves!

How to get things done efficiently

The part of the brain responsible for decision-making is the prefrontal cortex. It thrives in low-stress, well-nourished and rested periods, but it also functions optimally when we approach tasks with a plan, which involves:

- **small steps**, *doing one thing at a time, because this is the most efficient way to complete a task. Focus on doing the next most necessary thing.*
- **batched tasks**, *grouping similar tasks together and using the momentum from one completed task to move on to the next*
- **intentional breaks**, *setting a timer for 25 minutes and then taking a five-minute break*

- **minimal distractions**, *putting your phone in another room so you're creating a supportive environment.*

What you're doing when you write your to-dos on paper is closing mental tabs. A method for limiting distraction when you're at your desk is to only have three tabs open at once; it prevents you from flitting between pages and tasks – just another form of procrastination.

How to close the mental tabs

We expect too much of our brain. It's simply not designed to hold all the information we consume in a day. Our brain is designed to hold seven things in our short-term memory – anything more is too much, it's too heavy. And yet ask any woman, and she will most likely tell you that her 'mental load' includes far more than seven items. It's why transferring this load onto paper is a practical way of decluttering our mind that creates immediate space when we feel overwhelmed. This is a short-term solution. Ideally in the long term there would be someone close by who acknowledges this load and steps in to share it. But this is a much greater social issue, which encompasses the increasing demands and costs of modern life that are exacerbated by gender gaps (specifically in heterosexual marriages).

Remembering all the appointments, dates, details and to-dos of your life (and your family's) is not a sign of success, it's actually a major contributor to your stress. Take care of yourself by creating a system:

- *Write your to-do list in a dedicated place so you can easily access it and tick off or delete what has been done.*

- *If your to-do list is overwhelming, make it shorter by prioritising what's most important.*
- *Remember that done is good enough; we're not aiming for an immaculate life.*

The benefits of writing by hand

Handwriting is slower than our capacity to think and it's this intentional slowing down that allows us to hone our senses as we feel the pen in hand, watch the page fill with words, listen to the satisfying scrawl. It also helps us retain information in our memory. When we write by hand repeatedly, information passes more easily from our short-term memory to our long-term memory. Consider it a way of communicating to your brain that what you're writing is important and worth remembering.

When your brain is buzzing with thoughts and preventing you from switching off, journalling is a powerful de-stress practice that relieves anxiety and hones self-awareness. Research shows that it reduces activity in the amygdala, the part of the brain responsible for controlling the intensity of our emotions. There are no rules with journalling – it doesn't have to be 'good writing' or focused on gratitude or even legible. You do not have to write *Dear diary*. Think of it more as a brain dump. You know that satisfying sound when you empty the bin on your desktop? Imagine the same kind of satisfaction coming from the mental relief of getting all your worries, ideas, plans and regrets onto paper. Whatever is making you feel irritable, angry, confused or conflicted belongs on the page and out of your head.

FIVE WAYS TO ...
Restore your attention

1. Bring yourself back to the moment by focusing on your breath. Your breath is your one constant in life.

2. Be aware of how you feel. Remember that when you feel overwhelmed, your brain is telling you there's no space left. The remedy? Put your phone down, let your mind wander, resist distraction and spend time outside. This is the recipe for a mental declutter.

3. Weave small moments of joy and rest into your day so they become reliable habits that give you the mental clarity you need to be creative and productive.

4. Write a weekly meal plan. It removes the mental load of wondering what you'll make for dinner and is the most practical step to use what you've got and avoid waste. Cook double one night and freeze a serving; this is how you take care of future you.

5. Go on a walk and intentionally take note of what you see. Notice the light, the colours, the sounds, and remind yourself that next week they will be different. Nature is always changing and so are you.

9

Let your mind wander

It may look like a frivolous waste of time, but mind-wandering is the necessary work before the bright ideas come – the blank page before the creative spark.

Boredom arises when there's a disconnect between what we're experiencing and what we desire. It's not a nice feeling – it feels uncomfortable – but we can consider it a useful sign: our mind wants intrigue and action. In this discontentment, we can either procrastinate by distracting ourselves, or get curious about something.

Most of us 'digitally switch', which is the skittish behaviour of jumping between apps, videos or desktop tabs when we're bored – a form of 'fast forwarding' to speed up the distraction. Interestingly, this behaviour paradoxically intensifies boredom and reduces satisfaction and attention. It decreases the 'meaning' we attach to the practice, which inevitably amplifies our discomfort. We sink further into a dulled, frustrated mindset and we are left with frayed nerves and weariness.

Much like pain, boredom provides unpleasant but important feedback about our lives, telling us whether we want to and are able to focus on what we're doing. We can be bored for two reasons: what we're doing doesn't feel meaningful in the moment, or we can't pay attention because what we're doing is too hard or too easy.

If being busy is a badge of honour, boredom is a fine art. It can result in increased tension and stress, but it's also recommended for an engaged mind. Because allowing your mind to be bored, to wander, to do nothing, lays fertile ground for new and brilliant ideas. Indeed, if you're desperate for a spark of an idea, research tells us the best path forward is to get a bit bored. When we're bored, our minds tend to wander and passively explore – mind-wandering is an exploratory response to boredom.

Habits help us flow through the day without conscious attention, too. They mean we don't need to constantly make conscious decisions and can instead let our mind wander as we repeat the ordinary tasks we practise each day: brewing tea, loading the washing machine, walking the same streets, driving the same routes.

Have you ever sat in a doctor's waiting room or an airport or in line at your local coffee shop, and noticed the one person sitting and just looking around? Strange, you may think. They don't have headphones on or a phone in their hand, they're not writing notes or reading a book – they're just existing in their own space, observing.

Perhaps they're bored or maybe they want to see what's going on in the world and be lightened somewhat by the conversations they overhear, the connections between people they've never seen before and may never see again. It's a rare sight in a distracted world, but it's also rather beautiful. Do you have a longing for this kind of space, this lightness of being where you're not pulled and thrust from the beginning to the end of the day? I know I do.

What is exactly happening in the brain when we gaze into the middle distance, stop all the noise and think about stuff? Research suggests that we spend nearly 50 per cent of our waking hours thinking about something other than what we're doing. When we're thinking about anything but the present, our thoughts wander to what's happened in the past and what may occur in the future. Scientists believe that the wandering mind is also an unhappy one. But more recent research offers slightly more nuance, suggesting that mind-wandering can serve as an important foundation for creative inspiration, creativity, performance and wellbeing.

HARNESS YOUR BOREDOM

Have you completely removed boredom from your life? Most of us have, because distraction and stimulation live side by side in the palm of our hand, and putting down the phone to do something – anything – else requires focused intention and awareness.

Tolstoy described boredom as 'desire for desires', and cognitive neuroscientist Professor James Danckert says it's 'an aggressively dissatisfied state'. But social psychologist Dr Erin Westgate says it's simpler than that: 'It's just an emotion, like sadness or anger. You feel bored because you can't attach meaning to whatever you're doing (or not doing). You desperately want to be bothered, but you can't figure out how to ignite your interest.'

In 2014, University of Virginia researchers asked individuals to sit alone in a room for 15 minutes with only their thoughts for entertainment. Those who struggled could choose to distract themselves with an electric shock. The results across 11 studies were striking: most people said they hated being left to think – so much so that two-thirds of men and a quarter of women preferred to alleviate the boredom with a shock. Digitally switching is the everyday form of an electric shock.

Boredom is, essentially, being alone with your thoughts. In her research, Westgate has found that a lot of us really struggle to do this. It's not as easy to simply sit back and intentionally have a pleasant daydream. The discomfort of space is pronounced when there's no distraction.

Awareness of boredom is the first step towards harnessing it for productivity. And that's not a bad thing. Boredom forces us to break out of our routine and come up with new and innovative ideas. It is in this state of mind that we are more likely to take risks, experiment and try new things. Think of boredom as the precursor to creativity, the necessary step to broaden our thinking and stimulate ideas.

FIND FLOW

Creatives are constantly searching for inspiration – an idea, a sentence, a colour, a composition – and learning to sit in the nothingness is integral to a creative life. It's something we must learn along the way. Because when we let our mind space out and wander, we solve problems and do our most original thinking. Sit in boredom and you give your mind permission to wander off on all the tangents, each of which undoubtedly leads to new and surprising thoughts and ideas.

Science supports this. One study found that those who had engaged in a boring task before starting a creative one generated more creative solutions than those who did not engage in the boring task. Boredom is the push we need to make progress. But first, we need to surrender to it, and that's not easy because progress is an active process – there are no markers for mind-wandering. And our brain loves to know how far we've come and far we've got to go! And yet sometimes, boredom is the precursor to the state of mind known as 'flow', as described by Hungarian-American psychologist Dr Mihaly Csikszentmihalyi. He likened it to happiness in that it's elusive – it's not dictated by outside events but by how we interpret them. When we are challenged or engaged in an activity – totally absorbed in the rhythm of it and mesmerised as a result – we feel an element of control over our decisions and our life. These moments are known as 'optimal experiences' and they bring us closer to both flow and happiness.

You can find flow – which to me feels like a lovely consistent sense of ease and calm – whenever you're wholly engaged in an activity and oblivious to what's going on around you. You're protected in a membrane of sorts, a bubble of gentle thought. It's achievable for everyone, whether they're knitting, running, playing an instrument or pulling weeds in the garden. It almost feels like sinking into a slower brain pace, the opposite of frazzle. And this flow – of making and creating – is where the joy is. Flow doesn't exist in the finished product but in the process, because it's essentially about absorption, not accomplishment. This is clearly different from the happiness discourse that has us believe that once we've reached *x* and achieved *y*, we'll be happy.

Flow is not always a streamlined, positive experience, though. In fact, I think it's more to do with settling into the frustrating boredom, plugging your way through the metaphorical molasses and waiting for the rhythm to build, all the while working, working, working, intentionally engaging with the process and the problem-solving without being distracted. One 10-year longitudinal study showed that people in flow states are 500 per cent more productive.

For children flow is instinctive, and yet growing up in a world of distraction means it's potentially lost in a sea of screens. The exquisite beauty of a child sinking into their own imagined world is one of the most precious things to witness – talking to themselves, moving their body intuitively, unaware of time and social norms, lost in their wakeful dreams. There is something particularly innocent about it, isn't there? And perhaps that's what we crave when we feel as if our days are dictated by adulting: work, life admin and caring responsibilities. We want to return to a state of wonder so we can come back to ourselves, uncover a sense of purpose and cultivate hope in the world. Flow can give us that. Is this the crux of an abundant life? I think it may be.

Why does flow make us feel good? In a flow state, there is decreased activity in the prefrontal cortex, a process known as transient hypofrontality, which leads to feelings of time distortion and loss of self-consciousness. Flow is associated with the brain's reward circuitry, enhancing curiosity and engagement, hence it induces the release of dopamine, boosts wellbeing and acts as a magnet for learning, the development of new skills and challenges. I fear in the age of artificial intelligence, it's yet another endangered habit, because when we automate brain work, we reduce the desire to create and the rudder required to steer us through the work of it. Convenience dampens the challenge but it also likely removes the joy. And the joy that exists in flow is a private one; it's an internal jolt of energy that starts with a tiny spark that you follow, where you are less aware of yourself and of time, as you sink into the pull of the work. The experience is hard to define but Csikszentmihalyi said it well: 'The best moments in our lives are not the passive, receptive, relaxing times ... The best moments usually occur if a person's body or mind is stretched to its limits voluntarily to accomplish something difficult and worthwhile.'

Csikszentmihalyi described eight characteristics of flow:

1. *Complete concentration on the task.*
2. *Clarity of goals and rewards in mind and immediate feedback.*
3. *Transformation of time (speeding up/slowing down).*
4. *The experience being intrinsically rewarding.*
5. *Effortlessness and ease.*
6. *A balance between challenge and skills.*
7. *Actions and awareness being merged, so that self-conscious rumination is lost.*
8. *A feeling of control over the task.*

DO NOTHING

Just as the key to finding flow is to consciously attach meaning to the boredom, the same is true of doing nothing, especially if you're accustomed to always being busy and productive, and to tying up your sense of worth and accomplishment with what you ticked off the list today. When you attach meaning to doing nothing, it quiets all those parts of your mind alerting you that what you're doing isn't meaningful.

The art of doing nothing is called boketto in Japan. The Dutch call it niksen. Italians say dolce far niente – the sweetness of doing nothing. In English we refer to it as idleness, which definitely has connotations of laziness. These words are synonyms for mind-wandering – sitting or lying down and just letting your thoughts meander, letting there be yutori – space in the mind. Interestingly, both niksen and yutori have been applied to work culture. In Japan and the Netherlands, relentless productivity is a problem, so much so that in Japan they have a word for death from burnout: karoshi.

If you're thinking *I could never just do nothing*, perhaps you can start to see the purpose of switching off, giving nothingness meaning and then giving yourself permission to do it. The opportunity to slow down and reflect is so simple and accessible, but we tend to skip over it because there's always somewhere else to be or something else to do, always an excuse not to sit quietly and mull a bit.

A writer friend of mine has a daybed in her office. She knows when she needs to stop work and do nothing, so she'll lie down and inevitably awake with an idea or a solution to her plot problems. Often, it just takes sitting and gazing out the window or into the middle distance, lost in thought, resting in nothingness. I've done it a lot through motherhood, most especially in seasons of sleep deprivation, when I would sit in the rare morsels of space when no one needed me and just stare straight ahead, thinking of nothing. This is what comes to mind when I think of 'taking a breather'.

A brisk walk can also help – the rhythm of movement assists with untangling stuck points. Problems dissipate and eventually the answer comes. The unpredictable tangential nature of doing nothing is like untangling a knotted ball of string, neurologically speaking. Sometimes, holding string in your hand – weaving, knitting or knotting it – is a gentler path from busyness to nothingness, because keeping your hands busy gives your brain the opportunity to slip into default mode.

It may be uncomfortable at first, especially if 'busy' is your default, but consciously practising it each day, if only for five minutes, is one way to make it habitual. And just like yutori, there's no right or wrong way to do 'nothing'. There are no expectations attached to it, which is part of its appeal.

Doing nothing is, by definition, not meaningful. And that's why, when time is both scarce and valuable, we find it hard to justify nothingness. But doing nothing is actually something. It's subtly productive, because instead of being stimulated and distracted, we step into the stillness and space required to make sense of things. It's this stillness – being aware of and active in the nothingness – that differentiates it from boredom, which is often associated with a sense of dissatisfaction. This is where the subconscious has the space to join the dots with a degree of ease. It's a very different experience from sitting at a desk, willing and wishing for the answer to come to you.

> *You get to know yourself a bit better when you let yourself be. When we're not-doing, we're also unthinking.*

But thinking about nothing isn't a process that can exactly be described. I know if my children ask me what I'm thinking about it may take me a while to recall or I actually won't know. I'm so lost in the emptiness of my mind, I can't define a single thought. When I'm staring vacantly into the distance, my mind is somewhat absent, and this is boketto. It's not meditation because it's not intentional attentiveness – it's essentially about being blank. This 'space' gives the frontal lobes of the brain – the ones that deal with reasoning, planning and decision-making – the opportunity to recuperate and rewire so they can be the creative thinkers and problem-solvers. When we 'space out' we're creating opportunities for the answers to come. Cognitive insights arrive when the mind dissociates.

The brain's 'default mode' is also called the 'imagination network' – and I find it somewhat comforting to know that regardless of who we are and the doubt and fear that can get in the way of our creativity, we all have the ability and freedom to wander when our mind is not focused on an external task. If we follow the thought threads for long enough, we'll better understand ourselves. Being bored provides space to ask questions – *What now? What if?*, a step forward from *I don't know*.

Not knowing is uncomfortable, and the discomfort can force us to stay switched on because we fear wasting precious time. But what if the answers and solutions exist in the space we create when we effectively 'switch off' to do either nothing or something we can do while cruising along in autopilot – anything but what we think we should be doing?

The delight of an aimless wander

There's something inherently pleasing about pottering, which is to pleasantly move about without hurrying. I consider it the best thing in life: slowly getting the jobs done as you meander in your space, nowhere else to be and nothing else to do. More of this in life, please! Best done at home, no matter the weather, pottering is one of my very favourite things. I much prefer it when I'm alone (I'm unashamed of my delight in an empty house and particularly pleased when there's a reprieve from questions and requests). Sometimes I'll play music, I may light a candle, often I'll just listen to the stillness, which provides the perfect backdrop for a wandering mind and gentle thoughts. Pottering at home is a practical way to cushion ourselves from the world. And we all need that once in a while.

I also do it in the garden, where I pop out to check on the seedlings and feel so incredibly bolstered by the tiny shoots that push through from their cosy beds of soil. The garden is always teaching – fail one season, try again the next – but it's also embedded with optimism; from something so tiny, I can tend to a small sprout and in time, it graces my plate, sometimes making a whole meal. Of all the sweetness in life, a sun-warmed tomato picked from the vine and popped in your mouth is up there. I often don't plant tomato seedlings; they just shoot up from the earth, resurrected from the fruit that fell to the soil as the last summer faded.

Pottering is one way of looking after yourself. Perhaps it feeds the part of you that needs to step back and take stock, to have a bit of a cry or be angry or just mosey about if your head won't really let you do anything else. Sometimes you'll walk away feeling like it wasn't enough time, and sometimes you'll uncover a sense of peace, where the whirling mind has slowed, and quiet descends. It's in these moments that you'll come back to yourself; you'll remember what matters. And with this knowing, you'll move back into the world a little more grounded and more aware of how to care for yourself in meaningful ways.

TURN DOWN THE LIFE VOLUME

When we're inundated with information and entertainment, we have to make a conscious choice to turn down 'out there' and learn from the quiet 'in here'.

Sometimes it can feel like quiet is unattainable. Silence? Only for those who have retreated from the wider world to the realm of monasteries and ashrams, where conscious steps and hushed voices amplify every thought. Being in complete silence is uncomfortable at first. But practise for a few days and it quickly becomes normal. Return to the world and you will likely cover your ears, because it's only when something is removed and then reinstated that you understand the power of it. We live in a noisy world. And many of us recoil at the mere suggestion of silence because in conversation it's culturally awkward. But silence is where we access reflection. It's where we get to know ourselves.

The space between – the silence, the momentary pause, the interval, the breath – is a Japanese concept known as ma. It's the stillness when you wait for the kettle to boil, it's the pause as you watch the leaf fall from the branch to the ground, it's the negative space on a page between a chapter ending and the next beginning, it's the small gap between the inhalation and exhalation. It's intentional, contemplative stillness that is never considered awkward but a gentle gap in a life of doing. This emptiness is regarded as a possibility; everything changes, and if time and space are restricted there's no room to grow. Silence is ma, and rather than a void, it's seen as a fullness. It is absence, pause and silence. And in silence and stillness, there is clarity.

Sometimes we have to turn down the noise by making time to do what we really love. You know those things that naturally get pushed to the end of the list, the ones you only get to if you ignore everything else? The frivolous things that can often wait until later? If you make them wait, they get rather noisy.

Sometimes the quiet can be found in a single, slow moment that you recognise for what it is – a bit of space between all the doing. This space exists in the singular moments that accumulate: vacant staring out the window, sipping tea in bed, sitting on the back step to survey the garden or look up to the sky. This is what it means to *be*. It's also a skill that is being lost, yet there's immense value in it. You don't need to escape to a monastic lifestyle to access it, but you do need the discipline to sit there – in the likely uncomfortable well of quiet – without filling it with words or reaching for distractions. Sometimes this requires you to focus on your breath, the soft sound of it, especially amidst the chaos of family life and city living.

Seeking quiet in a noisy world

In 2018, Leighton Bradfield and Lockie O'Donoghue started 20Talk, an evidence-based youth mental health charity focused on mental health maintenance. They had lost two friends to suicide in the previous months, and chose to channel their own grief into making change. Their education programs normalise the range of human emotions and offer young people the tools and skills to integrate positive habits into their daily lives, bolstering self-awareness and dismantling the pseudo self-care that can often be a distraction. Fast forward six years and they rented out a warehouse space in Perth, Australia, for a fundraiser called 20 Hours for 20Talk. The premise was simple: invite 40 young people to sit together, in silence, for 20 hours. This was an opportunity for them to breathe and just be with themselves without being pulled away.

'We hear a lot from young people that they feel bombarded by life and by social media; they don't have space to rest or self-reflect,' Bradfield says. 'They often feel like they're mindlessly moving through life and not really experiencing it in a wholesome way at all.' This is reflected in the statistics: 44 per cent of young people say they feel stressed all or most of the time, and 42 per cent say they are personally extremely or very concerned about their mental health. In a 2023 American Psychological Society survey, about two-thirds of 18- to 34-year-olds said stress makes it hard for them to focus, and more than half considered their stress 'completely overwhelming' – most days they are so stressed they can't function.

Most of the 20 Hours for 20 Talk participants hadn't met before, but sitting in companionable silence there was an immediate sense of acknowledgment and love. This connection stemmed from being vulnerable, but sitting in silence without a phone is also a revolutionary act for Gen Z. As Bradfield says, their 'suffering' was evident before they eventually settled into stillness. They may have been bored and uncomfortable, but the practice was purposeful. When we live in a constant state of distraction we get lost – we lose sight of ourselves.

'It's like we don't really know who we are and that's deeply unsettling,' Bradfield says. 'I call it a transformative experience, because the external shock of silence helps people get back on track. I watched them tossing and turning, coming to realisations, journalling and eventually settling. It's wild how simple it is, but it's extremely profound.'

'Yeah, we're so distracted that we think the way out is really complicated,' I reply.

'Totally! And if you're on social media, you may feel the need to embrace some self-help practices, but every time you scroll you're literally inundated with lists on how to improve yourself and increase your savings. It's information overload and it overwhelms people. But you know what? We love the lists, don't we, but we rarely enact them. We're surrounded by other stories via social media. We're really questioning our own ability and confidence. Everything is so polished online.'

Bradfield believes that feeling overwhelmed is a consequence of an overload of information. 'People are so addicted to self-care but they never enact it and then they carry that sense of guilt and even shame that they "should" be doing more,' he says. 'It's heavy. What we're doing is providing the space to just sit – to think and be without anything else – and it proved to be revolutionary for everyone who attended.'

What 20 Hours for 20Talk provided was a safe space for young people to experience reflection and contemplation. Of course the discomfort of boredom came first, but afterwards there was the soft stillness of space.

FIVE WAYS TO …
Let your mind wander

1. Plan a potter. Turn the music on, light a candle, flick through a book, stare out the window, tidy a corner, take notes, check on your plants, sink into a bath.

2. Walk without headphones. Listen to the world around you and let your awareness meander as your feet do.

3. Swim laps. Diving underwater feels like a circuit breaker from the world, and the rhythmic movement following a single line softly focuses your awareness, which lets your thoughts untangle.

4. Pull back instead of pushing through and nurture yourself by tending to your basic needs – gentle movement, settled sleep and nourishing food. When you intentionally move slowly, you're creating space to let your mind wander.

5. Subtract the unnecessary. What can you let go of to create more space for what matters to you? Can you find gaps in your day where you can practise stillness and do nothing?

10
Walk the in-between

The ancient habit of walking can be the reassurance we need when we're stepping through liminal seasons.

Sea mist is my favourite weather phenomenon. When I see the barely there clouds roll inland down the street, I make my way to the sand so I can stand within the mist as it moves from sea to shore to the base of the mountain in the south.

Like breathing space, it's a shapeless form and no one knows how long it will stay before the conditions change and it's whisked away. This fog is like my mind in the moments and minutes after I open my eyes in the morning, not yet awake but no longer dreaming. It has no boundaries and it's hard to distinguish where it begins and ends. But what we know is that it's fleeting. In the early morning, when stars fade and the world is just waking, the brain is at its softest and most impressionable. How we spend the hour after we wake informs the rest of our day.

Essentially all of life is liminal, as we exist in the space between birth and death. But being in the in-between is innately uncertain and overwhelming. Our primal brain likes to know what's coming next. How do we carve out space and trust that it will lead to something positive? How can we get comfortable in the space in between? Liminal places exist everywhere: hospitals and airports, alleyways and hallways. The seaside town I call home is somewhat liminal – it's a place people often visit on their way to somewhere else.

Even the weather is liminal, as I stand on the shore and the sea mist blurs the line between sea and sky, land and cloud. My partner finds it eerie; anything could arrive on the wind without you knowing. Me, I'm just curious, because this mist, also known as fog or haar, is nothing but mystical to me. It feels full of possibility, a fleeting experience clouding the town so that, for a moment, it's as if we've disappeared. In her book *Chasing Fog*, Laura Pashby says: 'Fog is weather that becomes a space – somewhere that is neither here nor there.'

The sea mist rolls in and blankets the town and all of a sudden it's as if we're living in the clouds. The air is like gossamer, and when the sun hits it, it glistens because that's what happens when there is salt in the sky. This is the image that comes to mind when I hear the words 'soft fascination'. The mist is common in spring and summer when warm air meets the cold sea, when it's humid but you need to wear wool, when you can't see very far ahead and you wonder what's out there. A contradiction of a weather pattern can muddle with your mind but also floor you with its beauty. This is one of those moments of awe.

THE POWER OF WALKING

Liminality has to do with things that are neither this nor that, or perhaps both this and that, because they are transitional, in between. These life experiences are the wobbly ones that require patience and trust. They are softened, somewhat, by the ancient habit of walking. Because walking from one point to another is, in a sense, liminality, and the space between allows us time to reframe and reflect. But walking is more 'being' than 'doing', especially a gentle stroll that takes us through places and time and returns us home with fresh air in our lungs and a quieter mind.

One of my neighbours walks three times a day. I can see him from my desk as he walks past, collar of his jumper pulled up, cap pulled down. If he notices me he raises his hand and I smile, wave back. Walking doesn't have to be exercise, and while moving our body is always a good thing, I think we sometimes forget that walking allows a certain expansion. When we're not striving to raise our heart rate or work up a sweat, we can instead walk and notice and take in the details of where we live and who we live alongside.

Walking is not just about reaching a destination, it's about moving with the rhythm of life. Sometimes the body needs a quick and exuberant walk to get the blood pumping and the breath flowing – a tension release and limb stretch. And at other times, the pace is slower and meandering. We needn't rush when our body needs gentleness and time to wander. We need to let our thoughts be and our worries dissipate with each step; to amble without a destination in mind but with purpose, aligning mind, body and the world, as Rebecca Solnit says. It's a sure way to solve creative problems and sort moral dilemmas. As the Latin phrase says, solvitur ambulando, or it is solved by walking. Nature never seems to commit to one form – there are seasons and stages for a flower just as there are for us.

Perhaps this is why author and activist Jane Jacobs said that walkability was integral to a 'good neighbourhood'. She believed cities were for people, not cars, and resisted the urban sprawl that isolates those who live there. Instead, she was for converging pathways, because it's there that spontaneous encounters occur. When we stroll with curiosity, we are also more likely to chat with neighbours walking by, fostering a sense of connection – to people and place. It's this interaction that becomes the backbone of social connectedness and friendship. But walking also encourages introspection, an interaction of self. And for those who feel like they can't just 'do nothing', walking can bridge the gap between stillness and rest.

The route we walk is often the most efficient one, because this is how most of us live, in timeframes dictated by work schedules and school bells that require a certain pounding of the pavement. And that's okay – creating space is not about leaving your life but looking a little closer at it and making simple changes. Some days you'll be leaving home at the last possible minute to get to the school gate on time, and other days you may leave home 20 minutes earlier, to take a different route or amble your way there, because slow is your yutori.

When we go slower, we recall more details of the streets and landscapes than we would from being in the car or on the bus. It's these details that ultimately create a patchwork of memories. Think back to the apartments and houses you have lived in and the streets you have meandered along, the gaps in the pavement, the uneven paths, the rubbish and the rats, the graffiti and the buskers, the traffic lights forcing you to pause, the elderly neighbour waving from the front porch, the vintage chair or cast-iron pan that someone left on their front step because it was no longer wanted … and you stumbled upon it, celebrating its beauty and usefulness. And think of what you remember or, perhaps, what you have let be forgotten. Walking is solitude and also connection – be alone with your thoughts and keep an eye slightly ahead, looking to see where you're going.

Walking brings us back to ourselves because with each step we're reintegrating into our body, forced to be there, in it, and somehow the complexity of life isn't quite so oppressive. And yes, we know the value of walking through nature, but even in the high density of built environments, there is nature pushing through: dandelions, moss, fallen leaves, acorns. The trick is to walk slowly enough and train your eyes to see what's there, even if it's concealed. Because there is a hidden world beneath the one you're accustomed to noticing.

Silent walking

It's actually just walking, but it seems as though this simple act has been layered with expectations. Yes, you can go on a stupid little walk to improve your mental health (it does actually work), but without the earphones, athleisure and quick pace, it's a rare activity. And yet when we walk, we nurture a sense of belonging – in the body and the neighbourhood we inhabit. We have evolved to walk on two feet, but over time, with the ease of convenience and the accessibility of transport, we are slowly losing the need to walk. And with that, we are losing a part of ourselves.

Because when we talk about walking we immediately think of 'counting steps' – exercise to burn calories and shift weight and in some way improve who we are and how we look. But let's put that to the side for a moment and focus on what's most simple: one step in front of the other. Perhaps you amble or saunter, maybe you meander or stroll. Sometimes life dictates a trudge regardless of the surface beneath your feet, and other times you saunter because you feel a lightness of being and move easily through the streets like nothing is holding you back. Time slows down when we walk. It takes only 10 minutes of walking to boost our brain's happy hormones and neurotransmitters, which helps restore balance, regulate emotions and create perspective.

Walking is primal, something that many of us don't have to think about. But we need to learn to listen to our whole body beyond the sound of our breath and heartbeat. And sometimes, acquainting ourselves with our limbs is best done while walking through landscape, on uneven paths that require both presence and dexterity. Of course, you don't need to escape from your neighbourhood to walk. The best walk for you is the most accessible one.

In her book *A Walking Life*, Antonia Malchik writes: 'When we walk, we become something we've forgotten during centuries of technological revolution and the race to make our lives ever more efficient and productive – we become more human. And in walking we find the space to ask ourselves a question that perhaps we've been avoiding … What does that mean?'

It is the entire premise of this book – what does it mean to be human in a modern world, and how can we nurture our biological needs and natural processes? Walking provides the space to think and make sense of things; it's how we were designed to move through the world, reflecting on the landscape we exist in and responding to seasonal changes. If we are nature we make sense of ourselves by immersing ourselves in our natural habitat – the outside world. This doesn't mean we have to leave normal, urban life to do so. But it does explain our inherent disconnect if we have a mostly indoor, screen-based existence.

It's why a well-meaning person will encourage you to go for a walk if you are in 'fight or flight' mode – typically after an argument or a big emotional release. When the sympathetic nervous system is in control, the prefrontal cortex – the part of the brain that deals with reason – shuts down. This is commonly referred to as the 'amygdala hijack' – the primal part of your brain takes over, its primary purpose being to get you to safety. The amygdala's response disables rational thought and higher-level brain functions, leaving only the most primitive part of the brain engaged. You're not thinking, you're fleeing. It takes 20 minutes for the prefrontal cortex to switch back into gear, so going for a walk makes neurological sense. Knowing that you can't actually access 'sense', go for a walk. Let your primal body – the one designed to move as you trudge along the pavement – take over. As you walk, your adrenaline and cortisol will drop and your brain will slowly switch back into the mode where it can access sense, where you can listen and respond instead of react.

Moving gently through the world – with the time and space to breathe – may sound appealing. It may also look unproductive and perhaps weak – a waste of time, a squandering of opportunity. Softness doesn't mean fragility, though, just as strength isn't always a hard outer shell. Engineering researchers look to nature when designing materials for body armour and aircraft. What is strong yet flexible, sturdy yet whisper-light? Spider silk, lobster and abalone shells, toucan beaks, porcupine quills and seahorse skeletons. Nature provides templates not only for engineering materials but also for the human mind. 'Nature throws out metaphors right when you need them; it's a therapist, too,' says Dr Lara Bertolino, who takes all her clients outside for therapy sessions. It is there that the unyielding shell of a banksia pod, or weeds persistently growing through cracks in the pavement, or a bird tending its nestling, allow her clients to see their own experience mirrored in nature. The simplicity of nature helps us make sense of our own complicated, confusing lives.

Bertolino is a clinical psychologist who provides walking therapy for her clients, a practice that fosters a sense of ease for both therapist and patient. She takes each session outside – into nature – where winding, uneven paths, gumtrees, other native plants and birds create a softened, relaxed therapy space.

'Walking side by side is a bit more egalitarian, it's a bit less invasive or clinical, and it might help them,' Bertolino says. 'The movement or even just looking out to talk about something and then notice nature in between – all these things can really help certain people get more out of therapy because they use nature to regulate. I'm somebody who regulates in nature, so it helps me be a better therapist. I'm spending less effort and attention on trying to sit still and have an empathetic face. Outside I'm able to be more present and bring my full attention to the client and what they're dealing with.'

She admits that the dysregulation of being in a confined room, sitting still and obliged to make eye contact with someone who is sitting opposite her definitely hinders the therapy process somewhat. Psychology is focused exclusively on liminal spaces: big role transitions in life, major hurdles or traumas. Walking therapy brings the body and mind together; movement offers mental clarity. And being outside, making decisions on what path to take, is a learning process.

'In order to receive lessons from nature, you need to be outside and you need to be present to it,' Bertolini says. 'I ask my clients' permission to move between a traditional therapy session and observation of what's around us. Nature has stuff to say that's relevant; we can utilise it and tune in to it … Even the process of inviting and encouraging clients to do that helps them connect to their body and their feelings and what they're thinking. They may not be very in touch with what they need. I ask them, "Where do you want to walk, how fast do you want to walk?" And most of the time they'll say, "Whatever you decide." Over time they get better at knowing what they need and want. They may say, "I'm really tired today, I need to sit and be still," or "I'm feeling really stressed, so let's walk first and burn off some energy and then perhaps we can sit down at the end."

'Sometimes just being able to do different things in the space allows people to learn how to take care of themselves and choose paths that work for them where they can foster and nurture the connection between their body and mind. If the pathway is predetermined – sitting on a couch in a room – that learning doesn't exist for them. It's also an opportunity to self-reflect on patterns – if they're always the person that defers to someone else to choose, or they're running a million miles an hour without any awareness that they're puffed when they're talking … It becomes a non-confrontational, playful way to help people understand their patterns and what they mean, and how to play around with doing things differently as well.'

Of course, we don't need to be in therapy sessions to be aware of what our body and mind need and to move accordingly. Perhaps this is where 'exercise' has become a barrier, and instead we can focus on moving our bodies in ways that feel good and right in the moment. Stress and anxiety are dulled by consistent movement that releases endorphins and makes us sweat; walking on uneven surfaces – where we have to focus on each possibly precarious step – takes us out of our head and roots us in our body. When exhaustion is persistent, gentle movement can allow our blood and breath to flow without requiring excessive exertion.

How to be present when walking

The first and most important part of being present is being able to recognise how full your mind is. Sometimes we're not even aware of how busy our minds are, how distracted we've become or how much we're thinking about what's already been or what's not yet happened.

Bertolino says this is a great start: 'First, I'd give you praise for recognising that; you're aware now, you're present.' What can you do to cultivate more of that space?

- **Find sit spots**, *intentional places you go to in nature so your mind is free to process.*
- **Be intentional** *when you notice your mind is busy; don't fill it or distract it with more.*
- **Walk or drive in silence**. *We don't always need music or a podcast.*

My friend Laura (a different one) tells me about one of her favourite things: she drives to the small cinema that's 30 minutes from home and watches a movie alone. And then on the drive home she sits in stillness the entire time, thinking about what she's watched and what it means. This intentional reflection is one of the loveliest things about consuming art – the opportunity to really think about what we've read or seen or listened to and tune in to how it makes us *feel*. Art, if we let it, can alter us, especially if we approach it with the intention of looking slowly and mindfully at what it offers. This idea of 'slow looking' is remerging in art galleries and museums in response to modern life – quick-fire content and phones that so easily pull us out of immersive experiences and dull our senses. It requires patience and willingness, but the benefits are profound – improved mental health and increased critical thinking that leads to more meaningful thoughts. We can use this technique when we look at art and also at the world. Walk slowly and look slowly, and you'll begin to see so much more.

We don't have many gaps these days, we don't have a lot of breathing space because we're loading up with content. Our brains were not designed to have the world at our fingertips at all hours and with all the information in the world available to us constantly. Bertolino says that we do need to recognise that we're being bombarded and be intentional about turning away from it, carving out the gaps.

'It can be uncomfortable to do that,' she says, 'because we get dopamine boosts when we engage with content or you may be distracting yourself from painful thoughts or feelings. I think that distress tolerance and tolerating uncomfortable emotions – acceptance of boredom, discomfort, uncertainty – is critical, because otherwise we'll fill all the gaps. I think you need to accept that sometimes the gaps are uncomfortable.'

And yet it can be helpful to learn how to get comfortable there. If you have to stay where you are for 10 more breaths, what can you shift so you can be more comfortable? What would you change if you had to stay there for 100 more breaths? You can ask yourself this when you're in a challenging yoga pose or when you're strength training, when you're pushing through an arduous work project or when you're navigating a particularly hard season of life.

Create a sit spot

A sit spot is both a noun and a verb. It's a specific place to return to, somewhere in nature – a rock, a tree, a cove – to sit and observe; and it's also the practice of sitting still and quietly, observing and connecting without the obligation to document it.

Get used to the idea of doing nothing by allowing yourself unscheduled time. This could be as little as 10 minutes a week to start with. Sit spots might be a good way to start, where you go to the same spot regularly, sit down and mentally note what you see. I've unintentionally crafted a moving version of this by regularly wandering my garden and noticing what's changing. But I don't action anything – there's no pulling of weeds, tying of string or digging of dirt. It's just observing, which is another form of breathing space, an ancient habit that was vital for both survival and learning for most of our evolutionary history. If you're finding it hard to do nothing, a sit spot is a tangible step to stillness and, ultimately, to learning more about who you are.

TAKE A DIP TO RESET

The ocean is liminal – soothing one moment, treacherous the next – and while we can see it in front of us, there is so much below the surface that is unknown and uncertain. Salt water can offer solace – buoyancy, quiet, the impossibility of doing anything else but diving and floating.

In January 2021, Jude Abell refused to let another summer pass without swimming in the ocean. She lives in southern Lutruwita/Tasmania – a temperate island where the climate

is mostly cold and often wild – so she said to a couple of
friends, 'Let's just swim till the end of summer.' Five years on
and they're still swimming – through weather and seasons –
a daily rhythm that carries them through life and all the stuff
it challenges them with.

'It's always been a no-rules situation,' Jude says. 'You can
just jump in, you can swim a kilometre, you can wade to your
ankles. Nobody cares. In a world of rules, particularly for
women, this has been really important.'

Once submerged, a stillness descends, their minds quieten
and they gather together and look around. In midwinter, they
see snow on Kunyani/Mount Wellington and in autumn, when
the mornings are inky dark but the water is warmer, they'll be
electrified by the magic of phosphorescence. Every week there
is a subtle difference in the light. Often they will swim when
the sun and moon are in the sky, passing over. Observing this
marking of time, night becoming day, feels meaningful for the
simple fact that they're already out in the world, submerged
and immersed in the clarity of this time, the hushed tones
of waking.

Some of them call it swimming, others refer to it as dipping,
but they all experience the same body-bracing, mind-resetting
results, and it's changed how they live. Michelle Wild calls
it a 'deep dive into being', but before the relax and reset is
the hilarity. 'My body tingles! The slow walk in is crazy. We
often scream and yell and swear like wild creatures as the
moving water hits ever higher places on our bodies. We squeal
as the cold water hits our vulvas, and we obviously all have
different-length legs, so this never fails to make us laugh
out loud.'

'Dipping is low in energy input, high in outcome,' she
continues. 'I never regret a dip. I often do it three mornings

a week, and after a long day teaching high school maths and science I'll drive to my local waterhole on the way home to reset. I always feel better afterwards and I always feel a sense of happiness that I managed it, once again. So it is a reprieve from the world for my overloaded brain after work and the weeks of hard work. It's a great way to transition from work to home. I know this seems like an extreme method to reset, but teaching is stressful and the cold water is a perfect antidote. The effect it has on my brain is wonderful! It's a perfect way to stimulate happy hormones, and I can feel when these course through my body. I always wait for *that* feeling, then it's time to get out.' What she enjoys most about the weekly dip on Saturdays is the big group that gathers. 'I love being amongst the women, and feel strong in our solidarity of the cold-water dip.

'The effect of the cold water on my body and brain is profound. I feel quietly invincible afterwards. When I've been for a dip before school no one can affect my mood, everything just passes through and over and *out*. I am clear-headed, confident, calm, and most importantly have the space to deal with my students with compassion and positivity.'

Fine artist Dr Megan Walch explores the plasticity of thought and form in her work, and since joining Jude's swimming group three years ago, she's learnt that being in the cold water operates a reset: 'It makes everything okay again and my new high lasts all day.' She refers to herself as a 'cold-water dipper', but being in the ocean once a week for the past three years has been a vital space during a particularly pressing life season. Sandwiched between a mother dying of Parkinson's, a traumatised elderly father, a teenager and a sick husband, Megan was diagnosed with triple-negative, stage-three breast cancer three months after she joined Jude's swimming group. She started swimming because she wanted to be the kind of person who dipped all year round. This ancient ritual became a life jacket as she stepped day by day through gruelling treatment.

'I swam through much of my treatment, taking breaks during radiation so the salt wouldn't continue to burn my skin,' Meg says. 'I don't ever *want* to swim; I *have* to swim. For me, part of the practice is that it is always hard, but you override it. This practice of overriding discomfort bleeds out into other parts of life; you end up attempting other things that are difficult.'

'It's more a mental practice than a physical one?' I ask.

'My brain has become addicted to the rush of dopamine and serotonin. It can be blowing a gale, sleet falling, and yet I drive to my local beach, sometimes I jog for a bit and then plunge into the salty broth. My monkey mind has been short-circuited, thinking stops, I have risen above thought. This crystalline moment doesn't conform to chronological, linear time – it lasts a long time.

She describes this space in her mind as 'pure liberation in the cracks between leaden responsibility and grief; a timeless moment where I do something that's not habit'. Neurologically, it undoes functional fixedness, bolsters creativity and offers a sense of freedom. And if you are time-poor, Meg says a 'strip and dip' is highly effective. 'Sometimes I don't even have my bathers so I go in my underwear.' It's a jolt to bring you back to centre.

'Every week I know that if I need a connection I can join the group. I don't think I would have met many of these women elsewhere. The dipper diversity brings unexpected rewards and, as a permaculture fan, diversity is key to sustainability.'

Robyn Thomas has also swum while healing from cancer and navigating the depression that followed in its wake. It's now a daily practice that boosts her resilience. 'It makes me feel alive,' she says. 'Mostly I just keep getting up and going to the beach every day. I don't think ahead, I don't have a goal, I just get out of bed and turn up. It's a mix of crazy commitment and daily delight.'

She admits that everyone is so different, and yet at 6.30 am they are all wild women in the sea. And each day, in the same place, they look up from themselves and notice the subtle changes: turnings of tides and seasons, the change in the light, the micro-shifts that signal time passing.

'There is something very special about going to the same place at the same time every day and noticing the changes in nature,' Robyn says. 'No day is ever the same. You start to notice more – how high the tide is, where the sun pops up on the horizon as it moves in the season, how dark it is in midwinter, the shifts in the sand. In winter there is the wonder of a dark ocean and phosphorescence – slivers of light on the horizon.'

She used to struggle with seasonal affective disorder, where the last month of winter would mark her lowest mood. Now she skips into spring without hesitation; there's no more depression, depletion or exhaustion. Her daily swim – the push into the cold and the slow warming of her limbs, the tingling, the comfort of woollen clothes, the chatting over hot coffee afterwards – is just the reset she needs. 'Once I've swum I feel like I can handle anything that comes at me.'

As she says of any troubles or qualms: 'I leave it to the ocean.'

REVERE STILLNESS, BE TENDER

'Holding space' has become a throwaway means to wish someone well on social media, so while the vernacular is common, the intention is somewhat skewed. As author and facilitator Heather Plett reminds me, the ancient habit of creating breathing space for yourself is ultimately holding space, and that requires an element of tenderness. Space in the mind leads to softness of the body. Time may be racing, but it's also a precious resource. In this regard, breathing space needs to be treated tenderly.

'Largely when I work with people who aren't good at holding space for themselves,' Heather says, 'it usually comes from a place of all the expectations we place on ourselves, all the ways people expect us to show up, the expectations associated with the roles we have, whether that's mother, teacher, pastor – all of those expectations – what we have to start with is a noticing. It's being present enough to witness that you don't have space in your day, but it's also witnessing and acknowledging all those external pressures.'

When she considers holding space, she's exploring the meaning of liminality. 'It can be a directional move from one story to another, but it's also seasonal, and ageing is a liminal season – there's no clear beginning and end. And there's positional liminality, where some of us are living in liminal spaces all our lives – the edgewalkers, the storytellers, the people on the fringes of culture because they have a prophetic voice. I experience it in the queer space, and it's pertinent for people who are not living in the binary of male/female gender or heterosexuality; we're living in space that's not as defined by gender binaries.'

In her own research and experience, creating space and holding it – especially in liminal seasons where you're between 'what was' and 'what will be' – requires a certain amount of tenderness. 'We have learnt so many ways to treat ourselves that are not tender,' Heather says. 'So many of our systems – social, cultural, religious – have taught us to be productive and faithful, and the hard Ps of the patriarchy – perfectionism, performance, punishment, productivity. There are so many ways we harm ourselves and each other. In order to resist this way of being in the world, I needed something that felt strong and courageous but also soft. Tenderness is that word for me: soft inside your home but strong boundaries at the door.'

Tiny acts of care

Care is the safekeeping of oneself or another. In the small gaps that exist between doing all the things (or perhaps in lieu of doing all the things), choose gentle practices that nourish rather than deplete. Breathing deeply and slowly is the most accessible, wherever you are and whatever you're doing – releasing your tongue from the roof of your mouth, unclenching your jaw, softening your belly. You could also stretch and release your neck, have a bath, take yourself out for coffee and cake. Lean in to what's most comfortable: soft fabrics, nourishing food, songs that you know all the words to. If you have trouble slowing down in the in-between moments, look to nature: observe the sky, walk barefoot on the grass, tend to a plant, buy a bunch of flowers, let the sun warm your limbs, count the stars.

FIVE WAYS TO ...
Embrace the in-between

1. Revert to maintenance mode where the necessary jobs get done, even though they're not perfect. This season is not for striving, it's for taking care of yourself in simple, meaningful ways.

2. Recognise that you need stability more in this season, so lean on the habits that ground you – good food, sleep, regular movement, nourishing conversations with someone you trust.

3. Intentionally soften your body. It's really hard to move through the world gently, especially when you're in a period of profound uncertainty. Carving out moments in your day to soften your body is a powerful form of rest. Deepen your breaths, shake your limbs, release tension in your jaw.

4. Establish consistency with a regular bedtime. It doesn't need to be a multistep routine, but by intentionally slowing down and settling at around the same time each night, you create a reliable habit that you can lean on.

5. Create a sankalpa (a personal resolve or intention). In my own in-between seasons, I've relied on the repetition of a mantra to slow the anxiety spiral that can often stem from not knowing: 'I trust I'll land where I'm meant to be.' Create your own so you can rely on it when you notice you're overwhelmed and fearful.

11
Repair and make space

Resourcefulness and sufficiency are often countercultural – consider them a quiet rebellion. They are also timeless forms of therapy, bolstering our resolve and connecting us with community.

Sometimes we make space by repairing and making things. Crafting with your hands and whatever you have – thread, clay, yarn, pigment, pencil – requires your connection to the work you're shaping. You're focused, attentive and engaging in an ancient practice that connects you with all the makers who have come before you. And while we can generally buy whatever we need with ease, 'mending and making do' is how we've always lived. Creative pastimes aren't frivolous, they're resourceful, and they nurture in us a sense of purpose that gives life meaning. Paul Dolan, author of *Happiness by Design* says 'happiness is experiences of pleasure and purpose over time'. As humans we feel fulfilled when what we do has purpose. It's cumulative, too. The more we practise these habits, the more skills we gain, and the more resourceful and consumer-conscious we become – and the contentment that stems from this compounds. Is this the foundation of an abundant life?

Creative pastimes are also therapy of sorts. They bring us back to our body and our breath as we focus on whatever we're making, and along the way we return to an even keel. With each brushstroke or stitch, we release whatever has been bothering us. Repetitive, soothing movements along with a sense of accomplishment nurture a feeling of calm and contentment. This sense of achievement is a result of the reward centre in our brain being activated. A creative mind allows us to form new ways of doing things – as we work, we solve problems.

I come from a long maternal line of knitters, so perhaps it was ancestral habit to knit during my own pregnancies, to connect me with the mothers who came before me. The repetition helped ground me, because it's essentially a moving meditation: awareness focused, body still, breath deep. I experienced the same sense of profound stillness years later when Palawa woman Melissa West, a 'shell stringer', taught me how to make string with native grasses. She shared the stories of her people while I wove the grass. Now I weave at home and lean on this soothing practice to busy my hands and simultaneously slow my thoughts. In doing so, I create space for reflection. And that's precisely what allows the brain to untangle all the thought threads that contribute to feeling overwhelmed. When we're making something with our hands, our brain starts to clear out and take a backseat, and that's when we reflect and ponder. Working with our hands lets our brain take a breather.

The value of creativity is not the finished object so much as the process – the 'being' while 'doing', making space while we build, draw, weave or stitch. Some refer to it as mindful meditation, because the mental health benefits are profound, and so in a way, as you make things, you may also be mending yourself.

There is so much we can't control about our lives, but we can control our lifestyle choices: what we buy (and where we buy it), what we eat, what we wear. We want the stuff in our life to have meaning, because once it belongs to us, it requires our time. We use it but we must also care for it, protect it, maintain it. This is a responsibility, and that can feel heavy and make us feel stuck. We feel immediately lighter when we shed what no longer serves us – stuff and clutter, but also relationships and ideals. We are all living with profound excess; we have so much more than we need and yet everywhere we turn we're encouraged to consume more. Embracing simplicity and sufficiency is good for the planet, but often there's too big a gap between an individual's singular actions and their minuscule global effect. Instead, it's helpful to acknowledge, notice and experiment with the joy of less, the resounding sense of contentment that comes when you intentionally choose to go without, use what you've got and repair what's broken.

Because we're bombarded by the aspirational, it's so refreshing when someone shares the steps they took to pull back from a life that was consistently pushing them to their edge. In the rush of our lives, we're always looking ahead. If you admit that your life is stressful and if you've found yourself burning out, often the remedy isn't romantic. Sometimes it requires the ability to make space by changing *how* you live. If you want to create space to live a little slower and think a bit deeper, you need to get practical and accept that the money you make and the money you spend directly inform the time you have. Think of simplicity as resistance: it can sustain you when social discourse and political upheaval threaten to unsettle. Simplicity in its most basic form is space, because it gives you the freedom to live with less, which means you're not constantly striving.

This doesn't mean you have to feel guilty about how you spend your money. Instead, it's helpful to know that consumption is often passive – it's not so much an emotional response as a neurological one. Our behaviour is a reflection of the way our brain operates. If it's not rewarding, we won't do it. Our decisions are guided by an inbuilt reward system that has a vital function: it ensures we make choices that give us the best chance of survival. Your brain's reward system is not designed to make you feel good. Rather, it's designed to help you learn.

This system wasn't made for this time in history, but for a time when we humans didn't have much, when we were struggling to stay alive and had to learn how to do that. When we got food or shelter to aid this process, that would be intensely rewarding, and this was the encouragement we needed to keep searching for water, warmth and sustenance. The reason we get a dopamine release is to help us learn when something has a survival value. We didn't need to develop really big brakes to pull us back when we were overconsuming, because in evolutionary history our brains weren't designed for excess, they were designed for scarcity.

Mend yourself by making space

Sometimes it can be helpful to focus on one little patch at a time. We all have our problems, despite the fact that we may not share them with other people. Regardless of what anyone else says, you are an expert on your own life.

ENOUGHNESS

We live in a world that is all about bettering who we are and for one simple reason: our worth is defined by our ability to be economically valuable. The messaging to improve – the goal being 'greatness' – is persistent. But what we know about the psychology of happiness is that personal virtuosity is a slippery slope: the more we get, the more we want. As writer and psychologist Andrew Solomon says: 'The opposite of depression is not happiness, it's vitality.' A bouncing energy coupled with sparkling enthusiasm – for each day and whatever unfolds.

Looking at your belongings and deciding whether they are necessary is a process that requires both honesty and humility. You may think: *How did I end up here?* When you own less you gain a clear view of exactly what you have, which makes us wonder: what is enough? The theory of enoughness is rooted in Indigenous economics: take only what you need, leave the rest.

When we consider what's enough, we're ultimately figuring out what we need to live well. And yet so often we resist the elements that are necessary for wellness: space but also rest, sleep, nutrition, creative nourishment, connection, water, movement. It would be remiss of me to leave out a sense of security and the subsequent comfort of having a stable income, savings in the bank and a fridge full of fresh food. These things provide a mental buffer – literally space in the mind – even if we don't exist in a perpetual state of gratitude for them. But science also suggests that frugality is good for our mental health; there is an undeniable sense of contentment when we can stretch our positive experiences by savouring them.

There may be a social paradigm for success, but ticking predetermined boxes isn't a guaranteed path to a good life. After all, success doesn't equal fulfilment. Savouring life and everything in it requires the ability to romanticise, to see the good and wonder in the ordinary, to make the connection between beauty and the mundane.

For building designer Jane Hilliard, enoughness informs every aspect of her work and her life. She admits her home is not what you would expect of an architect and designer: it's a workhorse. Her family inhabits it differently depending on the season, and the mess represents the life – making, resting, being, doing – that unfolds within its walls. She is more concerned with having space for her garden, which by Nipaluna/Hobart standards is big – big enough for small but comfortable accommodation that she rents to people who are between homes. She doesn't use these words, but what she offers, in a nationwide housing crisis, is breathing space for members of her community. This small home borders her vegetable patch, which she refers to as her backyard supermarket – whatever is growing dictates her meal plan. The first thing she does each morning is go outside – where no one needs her – into the quiet and the green and, usually in southern Lutruwita/Tasmania, the cold.

In an industry fuelled by the aspirational, Hilliard is focused on the functional. Her career began in an architectural firm that labelled a new build as 'sustainable' if it had solar panels on the roof. But what Hilliard observed of the clients and everyone who worked on the houses was profound stress – budgets inevitably exploded, timelines expanded and no one was enjoying the process.

Now she attracts clients who envisage small footprints and intelligent design that don't cost the earth or all of their time. The industry would label her approach 'wellness design' and possibly 'ageing in place' – the homes she designs suit you now and will easily accommodate your physical needs as you get older. The home is, after all, where most of our resting and refuelling takes place; it supports us and also works really hard for us.

Hilliard encourages her clients to ask one question: 'What do we need?' and to let this dictate decision-making, as opposed to 'What do other people expect of my house? What's normal at the moment? What's on trend?'

It's a welcome change; one glance at social media and you're inundated with footage of new and beautiful homes – showrooms, effectively – and so many of us look at those videos from the mediocre homes we inhabit and sometimes feel less than. And yet our lived-in houses, with their chipped plates, familiar old lounge chairs and collection of miscellanies that we plan to sort through next week are the norm. And in their ordinariness, there is the quiet story of a life and, perhaps, a family. There is so much external emphasis on how the house looks, but it's helpful to consider how it functions, and also how you function in it.

When Hilliard is designing houses for her clients, an hour of work may look like a walk. When she returns to her desk, her subconscious has done the heavy lifting and she documents her ideas. Most of her clients are drawn to her because of her perspective: bigger isn't better, live within your means. She has been known to speak of only having one bathroom, an opinion that has triggered a lot of people. What does this say about us and our definition of 'essential'? We are so conditioned to abundance that we baulk at the suggestion of a house with one bathroom.

'Enoughness,' she says, 'is a lens for decision-making.'

But if we're even having this conversation, we're doing so from a foundation of privilege. There is irony in the fact that we're here with an abundant life, contemplating what is enough and shedding what we no longer need. And while we may be chasing perfection, it can be helpful to back-pedal a bit and be okay with what enough is – a more attainable and possibly more enjoyable 'good-enough life'.

'I think the best way to use it is as a lens,' Hilliard says, 'decide what things you want to have choice around and then let the rest go. We are thinking it's really important to make the right choice around every aspect of our life – for example, what drink bottle do we buy? It's actually not important and we don't need to take up space in our brain considering the options and making a decision. Using the energy to make that choice, find something in your cupboard that you've already got.' Her perspective is refreshing and it reiterates what we keep skipping over: in a world of abundant choice, we spend so much time and energy considering our options when we really could just use what we already own or explore what it feels like to go without.

'Enoughness is what you want to make choices around. What do you value? Your energy and your intentions and choices should stem from what matters to you,' Hilliard says.

And this process starts with one question: *Why?* When working with her clients, Hilliard asks these questions continually throughout the design process. And she's really honest about one simple equation: the more you do to your house and the bigger the mortgage is, the more time it's going to take from you because you have to work to pay for it. 'I always like to ask the question why. How are these home improvements going to improve your life? And if people don't have a clear, good answer, maybe they need to think about it a bit more.'

Enoughness and the brain

Here we are, looking for space, but there's so much in the way. We have to apply our own mental brakes, and the concept of enoughness can help. So, too, can language. American beauty journalist Jessica DeFino coined the term 'sale gaze' – the psychological condition of existing under capitalism where 'beauty' is synonymous with 'buying'. This potent gaze of wanting can be applied to anything new and shiny – all the things we lust over that hold the promise of making our life better.

Our brains also evolved to be rewarded by novelty, a preference that's been preserved in our genetic heritage because it gave us a survival advantage. Without it, we wouldn't have explored new things or been able to solve problems. This helps explain why, when we *can* consume, we *do*, even when we don't need to. We are biologically programmed to search out and acquire what's new.

If thrift is about the best, most efficient use of limited resources, enoughness is your mindset – knowing your worth, valuing time as a resource, being still in the moment, not chasing. The word thrift originates from thrive. Frugality isn't limiting, it's an ancient habit that actually expands your space, because without the mental weight of debt, or the resources required to keep up with trends and the constant looking ahead, you're more likely to focus your attention on right now – and know that it's enough. This is where we live – it's where we create. If we want a rich inner life with enough space in the mind, we have to be conscious of what we consume and keep, the stuff and clutter.

Even our collective drive to consume can be explained by neurobiology. This is where science is comforting, because it allows us to understand ourselves through a factual, evidence-based lens and not just a social one. We are primed to look for novelty because what's new provides a neurological boost in the form of a very real, albeit small, burst of dopamine. Every time we find and acquire something new, a positive response is generated in the brain. This creates a feedback loop that informs our decision-making and leads us quite instinctively down a path of consumerism. In a contemporary world of abundance, our 'scarcity mindset' – essentially, 'I'd better get this now because it won't be there later' – still clings to its ancient ways. And yet many of us are also intrigued by the concept of living with less – not because of necessity but choice.

Radical mending

'People are drawn to the concept of enoughness,' says Dr Ann-Christine Duhaime, a professor of neurosurgery at Harvard Medical School, director of paediatric neurosurgery at the Massachusetts General Hospital and author of *Minding the Climate: How Neuroscience Can Help Solve Our Environmental Crisis*. 'Simplicity is difficult to practise, and it was the core driver for my own research – the neurobiology of simplicity and why it's hard to simplify your life. What I came to is that you have to substitute other rewards for the rewards from consumption.'

Duhaime's personal choice is radical mending. It got its start at the Fashion Institute of Technology in New York, where if you had moth holes or wear and tear in the elbows of your sweater, they artistically mended it so it showed; there was no subtle replication of the original neatness. It's an ancient habit that's been revived globally as a form of creative resourcefulness and sufficiency. The French government recognises it as a practical way to avoid excessive waste (700,000 tonnes of clothing are thrown away each year by French people), establishing a €154 million fund to cover shoe and clothing repairs from 2023 to 2028. Customers can claim €7 for mending a heel and €10–25 for clothing repairs – a meaningful incentive.

'I became a radical mender and now I throw hardly anything away,' Duhaime says. 'I mend and make do and I show it off. It's almost become part of my identity. If something breaks at home, we mend it, even if it shows. The reward you're getting is the conscious acknowledgement that you're being more climate-friendly, but it's also imbued with the creativity process, the agency to fix something, the radical anti-consumption of it. There are neurobiological reasons enoughness is satisfying, an additional one being the moral sense of good.'

The ability to repair things can also be experienced as breathing space. When we engage mindfully with the intention of doing good, it can be a contemplative act. It's also a tangible connection: our head and our hands, our body and our breath.

If we are drawn to consume because of the novelty, it's helpful to redefine 'novelty' and use a biological lens rather than a cultural one. After all, 'new to you' is very different from 'new'. And while we are predisposed to seek novelty, we're not hardwired. Our moral priorities can inform our decision-making, and social rewards are powerful. When we find like-minded people making similar lifestyle choices, we're immediately bolstered, and this confidence reinforces our everyday habits, especially regarding how and what we consume. Science also tells us that when we find something pleasurable and can attach meaning to it, we're more likely to reach a state of positive wellbeing.

For Nat Mendham, founder of Mend Rebellion, which offers guides and workshops on mending in Nipaluna/Hobart, visible mending sits right at the intersection of art, resourcefulness and rebellion. It's given her agency to care for her clothes and reduced her need to shop (and her reliance on multinational corporations), allowing her to add new stories and new life to the clothes she wears and loves. It's also been the conduit to a slower, more considered existence, providing a slew of mental health benefits that persist for much longer than the stitching requires. 'There's the short-term dopamine rush from fixing something with your own hands, and because most mending projects are bite-sized, it's pretty immediate gratification,' she says. 'Long term, I think mending can help regulate your nervous system: you drop into a flow state as you make repetitive, slow stitches; your mind quietens and you become focused in the moment. I'm using my hands in a way that has a small but positive impact on the planet and that helps me cope with eco-anxiety and media fatigue.'

Finding space in creativity

Making space is not a one and done job. It's a life process that requires continual attention and care, and the ability to pivot instead of holding so tight to our ideals that we remain stubbornly stagnant. This is leaning in to rhythm, flow – it exists in the home, in the body, in the mind. And

in particularly uncertain times, we look to the most ancient
of practices for solace. What hasn't changed for decades –
centuries, even – feels the most reliable. Indeed, when you
feel as if the world is crumbling, there is meaning in knitting a
scarf, moulding a cup to drink something warm from, sewing
a blanket to curl up in – it makes you feel useful and manages
your anxiety. It bolsters your resolve so you can move on.
And often, embracing simplicity is a habit that, with time,
becomes your normal way of living, your lifestyle. It's not
something you have to think about, it's just something you
do – use up every inch of the vegetable in your cooking, mend
what's broken instead of buying new, choose less, unplug
appliances not in use, take only what you need. How do I do
it? Imperfectly but consistently.

For some, creativity takes place in the garden – watching
a tiny seed become a seedling and, eventually, leaves and fruit
that make a whole meal. And if you can't muster that, you
can at least find some grounding in the soil, its potential to
nurture – the plants within it and the person tending it. In this
way, the garden is medicinal. Gardens exist in communal plots,
neighbourhood sidewalks and balconies, too. A single indoor
plant is something you can take care of – observe and nurture –
if your space is limited but you still want to bring the outside in.
There's a woman in my neighbourhood named Faye who is in
her late eighties. She dances for 20 minutes each morning (to
get her going) before she spends time in the garden. She tells
me it's where she finds peace. Perhaps that's what we're all
seeking when we create and make and tend to something that's
growing – a feeling that everything will be okay. In this sense,
it's a remedy for prolific uncertainty.

Making as medicine

Just as we are meaning-making beings, we are innately creative, and it's a skill you can flex and foster as a means of coming back to yourself. In our most natural state we tinker and potter – gentle, creative acts of soft focus. It may be considered mediocre to relish in home – the comfort and familiarity of it, the tending to what needs to be done and the choice to spend time repairing and making things – but it's a potent form of medicine.

HOW TO CREATE BREATHING SPACE IN YOUR HOME

When we talk about breathing space, we're talking about the house we inhabit. Walk through the door, exhale, take off your coat and your shoes (and your bra); you're in your safe space … out of the life you live out there and into the reprieve you've created in here.

'Breathing space is something everyone craves and is hoping that their homes provide, and they probably should,' Hilliard says. 'I think literally, from a design sense, you need to focus energy and thought on the service areas of the home and make them work really well. And make sure the flow of tasks and processes that happen in your home are catered for to make them easy.

This looks like a designated transition space for your belongings that you use for work and activities outside the home:

- *a bowl or hook for your keys*
- *a mudroom, wardrobe or hanging rack for shoes, bags and coats.*

'When you have a transition space so you can leave things there, you leave the outside before you and pass through a threshold into your home, where you can relax and feel nurtured and not have the pressure of the world on you.'

In a kitchen, for example, make sure everything has a place. Think about the process of preparing food, eating and then cleaning so that's easy. Make it a nice space to do it in so the task gets done. Same with washing. Our homes, while they do need to give us breathing space to relax and recharge, also function, and they have to work so we can get tasks done. Zoning your house into work space and relaxation space is helpful – try not to cross them over too much.

This looks like:

- *not taking your phone or any work into your bedroom*
- *keeping what benefits you and passing on what detracts from a sense of ease*
- *prioritising the practical in your 'work' spaces.*

Let the air in

Airing out your home – even in the middle of winter – is a Nordic tradition that's been practised for generations. Opening the windows and doors for 10 minutes a day in the cold months is a quick and effective way of creating more space. It connects you to the season, improves indoor air quality, and boosts your energy and mood. Do it in the morning when you're getting ready for the day and you're keeping your body warm by moving about.

Less work, more space

Creating space is about subtracting the unnecessary. This requires consideration of what's essential, and this naturally leads to ruminations on priorities and importance. It's a path that quickly prompts you to unpick your week – the schedules and appointments and time blocks in your diary – and weigh their ordinariness against your values: *What matters to me?* You may ask, *What do I care about?* Is this the very crux of an existential crisis, where you consider who you are, what you're doing and the meaning of life? Perhaps. It can also be a productive way to reshuffle your priorities so you spend more time and energy on the things you care about, which naturally alters your perspective on the space between.

Change starts by asking questions, and for freelance journalist and permaculture practitioner Koren Helbig, the first question was: *What can I do about this?*

'My sister and I both realised we were in these corporate jobs that didn't feel very aligned with who we were and what mattered to us, so we started asking questions,' she says. 'We were living in the city at the time and I was working ridiculous hours every week. I realised that I was rarely stepping outside because I was on the computer from early morning till late at night or commuting on the train. And because I'd lost that outdoor connection so gradually, I had barely noticed that I was now living a mostly indoor life. It wasn't aligned with who I am; it wasn't making me happy.'

Their solution at the time was to imagine a future where they were living aligned with their values, where their work was shaped around their life. But they weren't exactly sure how to get there so they started a blog, which morphed into a podcast, where they spoke to women who were where they wanted to be. 'The women we were talking to were working part time, or self-employed or had left behind high-flying corporate careers to do something intentional but unexpected – like live in a forest for a year,' Helbig says. 'That was where we really pushed the boundary of what we thought was possible, by talking to people who were already there and were like us – in their thirties, having a go. They hadn't figured everything out, but they were trying.

'We talked about the little changes we were making in our lives to get to where we wanted to be,' Helbig says. 'They were visible markers and every step was a celebration. It was simple stuff: shopping second-hand, making more food at home, growing herbs in pots on the balcony. I was vegetarian at the time, so we spoke about the food system from the perspective of, can we champion plants in meals? We were living in a little house in Meanjin/Brisbane and didn't feel like we had much agency, so we really focused on those small, actionable steps.'

And small, actionable steps that can be applied to your life – regardless of where and how you're living – seem to be a tangible move towards making change and creating space.

It reminds me of Anne Morrow Lindbergh, who writes in her book *Gift from the Sea*, 'But neither is the answer in dissipating our time and energy in … more accumulations which supposedly simplify life but actually burden it, more possessions which we have not time to use or appreciate, more diversions to fill up the void.'

On her email signature, Koren Helbig highlights her working days (Monday to Thursday). She's consciously chosen to work part time, even though she has a mortgage to pay and lives in the city. All her lifestyle choices, from working part time to being self-employed and living in a 100-year-old house with a small garden, have been thoughtful ones. You could say she views life – and living – through a permaculture lens, where she has created intentional breathing space for herself.

The former political journalist has not always lived like this. And perhaps that's why she's the best example of change: she figured out the steps she needed to take to live intuitively, with ample breathing space available to her, and she set about making it a reality.

'I wanted to subtract this career from my life,' she says, 'but in order to be able to do that, there had to be an incubation period that was really internal, or at least in my internal circle – my sister, my family and a few choice friends who would support me and build it up.'

'Your fragile idea needed breathing space to grow strong?' I ask.

'Yes, exactly that.'

But even turning that idea into concrete plans needed breathing space to come to fruition, free from the opinions and assumptions of others. 'My idea needed to be more solid before I told many people about it,' she explains. 'Similar to when you germinate a seed inside on the windowsill before you transplant it out into the weather to harden off.'

Her idea is now a reality, and she admits that the smallness of her city life has created the opportunity – and the space – for mental, emotional and energetic reprieve. 'The house is small, 87 square metres. The block is small – 478 square metres. I knew they wouldn't be onerous or expensive or time-consuming to care for, which would allow me to have breathing space – rest, connect with my wider community, do other things.'

So what does breathing space mean to her? 'When I think of breathing space, I'm not only thinking of resting time, but of things in my life that help me to feel generally calm, because that's what allows me to feel like I have room to move,' she says.

'It's all about doing it your way, and often that means consciously stepping to the side – which is hard, because you're watching everyone else carrying on ahead of you – and trusting that the small steps you're taking are in the direction that feels best for you. There's fear of missing out and also fear of failing to keep up, but that's actually a good question to ask yourself: *Who am I keeping up with? And do I really care?* Of course, there's also the opportunity to find more joy and contentment when you do things your way, and it's likely you'll also connect with plenty of people choosing to live the same way.

Helbig creates balance between work and rest, is clear about what she wants, and has spent the past decade in pursuit of less for a life of more, honing her skills so her lifestyle embodies and reflects her values. She lives in a small house with an abundant garden, a cat and a small brood of chickens. She's chosen to live frugally because it gives her autonomy. Quoting Alys Fowler's *Eat What You Grow*, she refers to her rambling garden – a place she has planned and tended for three years – as her 'wild bit of the world', her 'tiny slice of reciprocity with nature'. Her life (and her work) is rooted in the pillars of permaculture: a self-sufficient lifestyle where resources – food, heat, light, energy, time – are valued and used mindfully.

So how did she plan to work part time? She got practical. She, like Jane Hilliard, knows exactly how much she needs to earn to *live well*, and that's exactly how many hours she files into 'work time'. It's a clear boundary.

WHAT CAN YOU SUBTRACT?

Sometimes simplifying and creating space is all about what you *don't* do. What can you let go of?

It's not an easy question to answer, because when you ask these personal questions of yourself they naturally prompt insular thoughts – a private and perhaps indulgent process that requires a certain level of privilege. But creating space is not ignoring or turning your back on the world, it's simply stepping back and seeking momentary stillness so you can ultimately move forward again with renewed energy, so you can see the world more clearly. Guilt can easily become a barrier here – guilt for this self-consideration, this intellectual navel-gazing, so to speak. And yet when you choose to live with less, to make physical space and be mindful of not filling it back up, you're creating time, too. Space begets space, because you don't have to work as much to buy the things that you no longer need. And this carves out time for the things you love, which may be doing nothing or creating something.

Subtracting the unnecessary, getting comfortable in the not knowing, choosing not to explain – this is how you create space. Of course, you can declutter your home, too. Fill a bag with books you won't read again, clothes that no longer fit, the extra

10 coffee mugs you own but don't use. This sense of making physical space to create mental clarity is the foundation of traditional Japanese aesthetics, which informs minimalism – in negative space you find potential. But minimalism in our homes isn't always practical or possible. We all live in the mess of life, many of us with families who may not share our desire for clean surfaces and tidy corners. Life is inherently cluttered – with schedules, to-dos and obligations.

But it never hurts to consider clearing out and carrying less. Thinking about what you need to live well and how you can learn to live with less clutter. Creating physical space in your home to make space in your mind. Clearing whole days in your diary to create opportunities for spontaneity and meandering. Reframing 'stepping back' or 'stepping down' as a productive step forwards. I liken this to subtracting the unnecessary, taking away the stuff I no longer need and being mindful enough to prevent it returning.

FIVE WAYS TO ...
Repair and make space

1. Consider the currencies of time and money. Everything you buy costs money and time, so when you're considering a new item, resist the impulse to buy and write it down in your diary. Wait three days. Reconsider whether you want and need it. This is how you consciously consume.

2. Set a timer for 10 minutes. This is helpful when you feel like you're behind on all the necessary chores but you don't have the time or capacity for a big clean. Start small, focus on one room, be intentional and get the job done: clear the bench, sort the tiny piles of miscellany that have gathered, put everything back where it lives.

3. Unsubscribe from marketing emails. They clutter your inbox and also tempt you to buy what you probably don't need.

4. Declutter one drawer. This is how you start to declutter your house. One little space at a time means that you can do it efficiently while also having the clarity of mind to make decisions about whether you want to keep or donate something.

5. Outfit repeat. Let's normalise wearing the same clothes over and over again, because it removes decision-making, frees up time, decreases the washing pile and prevents us from contributing to the fast-fashion waste crisis.

12
Build space to create

If we want to live a creative life, we need to schedule rest and mind-wandering. They are a vital part of the creative process and should be valued as such.

Schedule the habits of rest, mind-wandering and creativity just as you do social gatherings and doctor's appointments. This is how you get practical and make consistent change.

Sometimes we have to turn down the noise by making time to do what we really love. You know those things that naturally get pushed to the end of the list, the ones you only get to if you ignore everything else? Those frivolous things that can often wait till later? If you make them wait, they get rather noisy.

Creating and making quiets the mind.

Quiet work

Reading and writing, stitching or drawing are quiet work. The simple, ordinary act of using your hands slows down your thoughts. Creating isn't so much about the finished project but about the sacred space that opens up before you (and around you, it feels like). When you're sewing on a button or handwriting a sentence, it's like you come back to yourself; you exist in a bubble for a small moment in time.

This is flow, isn't it?

Afterwards, instead of carrying the frustration that you're not tending to your imagination and moulding and stretching it in the way it's begging you to, you move through the day knowing that you nourished yourself in response to the soul-calling. It feels like a contented exhale.

CREATING SPACE FOR CREATIVITY

I wrote most of this book while walking – no pen in hand, no phone open to the notes app. I've come to know this time as my most productive, an emptying of the mind so I can let go of the grasping and instead allow the thread connections to bubble up. The active part of the process is my ability to carve out the space, like a weeding of the garden, ridding it of the distracting dandelions and inconspicuous tendrils to create a fertile patch. And then I sit quietly, watch and wait. At the desk is where I come back to myself, and as I figure out how to write my thoughts, as I learn the connections and the rhythm of whatever I'm writing, I learn a bit more about myself, too. Creativity is, for the most part, self-discovery.

Australian jazz pianist and singer Monique diMattina says, 'We need to build a cathedral for our stillness.' Author Charlotte Wood envisages a circus tent for her creative work in *The Luminous Solution*. They are cavernous spaces – one holy, one magic – both deserving of reverence because stillness is as sacred and vital as breath and heartbeat. Breathing space may exist, but being still there requires even more of our intention.

'This stillness doesn't happen just anywhere,' says diMattina. 'We need to make effort to carve a space for it. I carve space in the calendar, turn off the wi-fi, but also make effort to sculpt myself with activities that make me resonant. Gardening. Meditating. Long walks. These things get me in good shape to receive sounds.'

Creativity is a refuge and also a resistance. And we can find ourselves, more often than not, fighting for space to create, dreaming of days where there is nothing but time and opportunity, and then getting frustrated by the lack of it. And yet ask any writer, most of whom juggle a job of some sort with their writing, and they will tell you that while time is important for creating, don't underestimate the opportunity of 25 minutes or an hour. Writing a novel doesn't require great swathes of time but the discipline to schedule minutes and cradle them so they don't get whisked away by shouty obligations.

While I don't feel more confident as a writer, and I've come to accept that the uncertainty of creating is quite a useful part of the process (it ensures I keep looking, keep turning up to figure it out), understanding how my brain functions and what it needs to be present, calm and engaged, has allowed me, for perhaps the first time, to find some semblance of work–life balance. I never switch off the writing part of my brain, although I know that my writing self is not my definitive self. But knowing that breathing space – rest, non-doing, mind-wandering – allows it the time to restore so it can be calm, alert, present and focused, means that I value these practices as an integral part of a creative life. They are the work.

I now know why I experience a burst of creativity after a walk or a swim: I've set the problem aside and I've let my brain rest. It's this exposure to and immersion in the natural environment that restores my directed attention and improves my ability to think, solve problems and create.

Switching off the left side of the brain

The brain requires rest to recharge and refuel. When we allow ourselves to rest, we switch off the left side where the rational day-to-day thinking happens, and access the right side, where creative, intuitive thinking occurs. It's here that the aha moments, insights and curious optimism exist, the thoughts that eventually lead us into creating.

I realise that I'm at my most productive when I'm not sitting at the desk, when I have consciously turned away from the work – and the pressure to create – and instead open myself and my senses to whatever may come. For writer Maggie MacKellar, it's work on the farm: 'I'm digging a load of sheep manure into the vegie patch when J calls over the fence, "I thought you were writing?" I yell back, "I am. This is what writing looks like."' Author Hilde Hinton builds Lego between paragraphs; building blocks builds plot, too. They're not looking for answers in sheep shit or vivid plastic rectangles, but they know how their brains work – that there is something incredibly useful in switching off the thinking part of their brain and working with their hands, paying attention to the colour and texture and conversations of the world well beyond the blank page. That paying attention to the ordinary, attending to everyday life and then bringing those observations to our work, is how we make sense of the world – how we make sense of ourselves.

Writers Helen Garner and Abigail Thomas – both in their eighties – have spoken of the space they sit in, waiting for an idea to come. 'I've been at this long enough to know there will always be the next [interesting] thing, but I need an open mind,' Thomas writes. 'Sometimes it shows up in disguise, a bug, say, or a particular shade of blue, a joke somebody made that wasn't funny. And when I feel that tug, especially if it makes no sense, I pay attention.' Garner admits that interest is enough: she's 'always waiting for something to make me feel like I'm busting to write about it'.

Attention, mindfulness and curiosity

Not far from the white cliffs of Devon, in a small rural town, artist Alex Boon tells me about nature journalling: notes from the field or the beach or the meadow. Wherever he goes, he carries his kit with him, chooses a spot to sit, and spends hours observing and documenting, nurturing a kinship between himself and the natural world. It's this practice of quiet and deep noticing that fuels his art, but it's also his meditation. As a student of Zen Buddhism, he has witnessed the merging of his meditation practice with his art and naturalism, and the result is a deep and beautiful documentation of the sky, seasons and sea, and the flora and fauna he notices throughout the year. He writes, draws and paints what he sees – robin, mushroom, nettle, stone – fostering a deepening awareness of the seasons and the tiny, almost imperceptible changes that occur in the shifting of seasons and time: gull, field, oak, shell.

'I'm deeply connected with the seasons because it takes you beyond what you think the seasons are,' he says. 'We start with a really clear idea: spring begins when the frosts ease and the flowers start to bloom, autumn begins when the winds come and the nights draw in. But what nature journalling does is make you look for spring in winter and summer in spring, and you start to notice a merging of the seasons. There's so much overlap, especially with climate change and species loss. I've also noticed the change from year to year and how blurred those once distinct seasonal lines have become.' He has detected a lull in nature's sounds, too; the world isn't as naturally noisy as it once was.

Boon marks season and moment with his pencil, in a notebook that is both detailed and vivid. He tells me his practice began when he moved from the commuter belt in London to the West Country, settling in a small seaside town where green fields drop into white cliffs and down to the sea. But his journey to breathing space started years before, when he was diagnosed with seasonal affective disorder; not enough light exposure resulted in lethargy and depression. He set out to explore his new area and started documenting what he found. It was years later, when he shared his work on Instagram, that someone suggested he tag his photos with #naturejournal. 'I had no idea it actually had a name and that there was a whole community of people around the world doing it, too.'

Nature journalling is a tangible way of paying attention. It requires you to get outside, sit quietly, observe, notice – to keep looking – all those things we're not very good at, generally speaking, in a bright world that requires megawatts of energy.

'We are what we practise, we're creatures of habit,' Boon says. 'If you spend all your life doing one thing, you're very practised at being a certain way. Ever since I've started nature journalling, I've created a deliberate, consistent practice away from an internet-based, fast-paced way of living. I suppose you could say I've created breathing space for myself, and I can't imagine my life without it now.'

He writes and draws and chooses not to place too many rules on the practice. 'The first time I went out, I just decided to walk a long-distance trail near me and I took a book with me and described the walk as I went. After that project, I took my book whenever I was going out on a walk. It didn't have much direction at all and I didn't have a barrier up – I didn't call it a nature journal per se, because I didn't want to only write about nature; I wanted to write about whatever came up. If I was feeling a bit down, I'd write about other things as well. I wasn't keeping a diary, but I wouldn't exclude my feelings from the place I was documenting, either.'

Now he tends to sit in one spot for a period of time, a practice informed by meditation. 'Buddhism has influenced and deepened my nature-journalling practice,' he says. 'Rather than walking and writing, I'd stay in one spot, listing what I could see, trying to go deeper and notice more, even if it didn't look that exciting from first glance.' He practises the precision of a naturalist (he is an environmental scientist) with the freedom of an artist. And part of that is not glancing at an object and letting his brain fill in the blanks; it's holding his attention on what's in front of him and looking at it carefully, noting the texture, colour and shape from every angle, what it does in light and in shadow.

'What did it teach you?' I ask.

'Mindfulness. I study a type of Korean Zen Buddhism called Seon, and that has a question you meditate with – *What is this?* – and you sit on your cushion and continually ask that question and it becomes introspective. The challenge is to stop it becoming analytical. I ended up struggling with that question so I changed it to *What else is here?* – and that question became

the most important part of my nature journalling and how
I teach it.'

This is slow looking, which informs the act of savouring –
paying deep, careful attention to the world – and right now
it's countercultural, because we're accustomed to skimming.
Psychologists believe slow looking is one key to happiness;
it stimulates the brain's reward centre and can reduce the
symptoms of depression. What Boon can't teach is curiosity,
but he knows that it's sparked by being outside and letting
go of the barriers that prevent us from questioning. Science
also tells us that this questioning, which prompts heightened
awareness and inquisitiveness, assists with memory retention.

Charlotte Wood, in her book *The Luminous Solution,*
calls this 'digging and diving' – going beneath the surface of
things to find meaning. She's referencing the creative practice
specifically, but this premise – of being curious, foraging for
clues and seeking answers – increases the neural activity
in the brain circuits that release dopamine, the feel-good
hormone associated with focus, reward and motivation (and
addiction).

Curiosity is considered the noblest of human drives, but it's
also dangerous (curiosity killed the cat) – too much of a good
thing leads to distractibility. But then diminish the curious
drive too much and you have a symptom of depression.
Curiosity is not only a human trait; it exists in all animals, even
the humblest of worms, to ensure survival. And while curiosity
is vital for childhood development – the abject amazement
at the big and the small wonders – research shows that it's
essential for adults, because it helps us understand the world
and who we are in it.

Taking field notes

Nature journalling is documenting local knowledge, but it's also a conscious stepping away from home and screens, and a tangible way of deepening your awareness of nature, especially if you feel that life is detaching you from the seasons. Start by walking and noticing, really paying attention to what's around you, whether you're on a sparsely populated rural path or an urban park. The people who are most attracted to this practice are those with a similar way of being: bookish, introverted people who already have a strong love of nature and want to deepen it.

72 micro-seasons

According to the traditional Japanese almanac, the year is divided into four major seasons, 24 sekki (solar terms), and 72 kō, or micro-seasons. Each kō lasts only five days and is marked by a subtle newness in nature: the emergence of a sprout, a bud opening, the ripening of fruit on the tree, the first sighting of swallows after the winter. The very nature of these fleeting seasons – and the length of them – requires a consistent noticing, and the promise to step outside each day and pay attention. But these short seasons also create a steady, reliable rhythm, and there's comfort in being reminded – every five days – that life changes; nothing stays the same.

Each kō draws you into the moment, and this practice – fostering an awareness of the season, albeit brief – is known as kisetsukan. It's spring when I learn of this calendar, which isn't solely a Japanese practice. Ancient cultures (Egypt, Babylon, Greece, China) looked to the sky – the phases of the moon and the scattering of stars, the fields and the trees – to measure and mark time, and Indigenous cultures still do. The Japanese calendar is inspired by the seventh-century Chinese one that subdivided each year into moments: 'peach blossom' to herald the first warmth after months of cold, 'white dew' for the beginning of a descent towards the shortest day of the year.

In Lutruwita/Tasmania, the winter wattle – a native flower reminiscent of small yellow pom poms – erupts suddenly across the valleys like a golden curtain heralding spring. Look closer and the daffodils are there, too. And then a few days later, the cherry blossoms and finally, when the daylight lasts a little longer and there's enough sun on the tree, the magnolias unfurl from tight buds. Months later, I notice the tip of the first leaf on the Japanese maple outside my window fades to yellow. It is the tiniest change, minuscule really, but because I noticed I feel somewhat connected – and prepared – for the days and weeks to come, when all the leaves follow the same pattern – green, yellow, orange, red – before they fall to the ground, dampened by the rain and disintegrating in the frost of a fallow winter, where the days are short, the earth is quiet and we retreat to the comfort of home to recuperate.

It is a constant change, a persistent hum, a reminder that everything is connected, ourselves included. These incremental changes measure the passage of time ... We may be dedicated to our days and schedules and to-do lists, but we can also notice the sound of our breath and footsteps as we walk through the neighbourhood, learning and connecting with what's alive – growing, receding, sprawling, retreating. Walking in your local town or neighbourhood can be everything but routine – it's fragmented and endlessly absorbing if you walk *and* notice.

Slowly looking at the world

We are shaped by where we live, and Boon's experience of nature journalling is a means of deepening his knowledge of the world around him and, in turn, fostering a deeper understanding of who he is on the land.

Learning something new – anything new – forces our brain to be present and focused. Time actually slows down in this newness, which explains why childhood is subjectively slower than adulthood. Back then, we were learning something new every day, but when we slip into repetitive habits and routines, we don't have to be so present, so we do it on autopilot and our mind wanders somewhere else and we say to ourselves and each other: *Where has the week gone?*

One of Zen Buddhism's teachings is 'Not knowing is most intimate', which naturally leads to a confidence in saying 'I don't know' and to realising that the purpose is not to find the answer but to sit with the question.

Being in nature – whether you're documenting it or not – is what we're genetically programmed to do. Biologist Edward O. Wilson developed the biophilia hypothesis, a theory that says we have an ingrained calling to be in nature but it's in competition with our inate need to control our environment.

Remember, the brain loves predictability and nature is becoming increasingly unpredictable. And yet we forget the most basic fact – we are nature – and when we're not regularly exposed to green and blue open spaces, we are affected and essentially depleted.

Convalescing in the countryside has long been a form of remedy. Sea air awakens the senses and instils a sense of calm. Indigenous plant medicine is a potent healer. But science hasn't always supported the belief that nature is physical therapy and mind medicine. That is until the Japanese Forestry Agency created a nature-based wellness program in the 1980s that promoted walking through and 'taking in' in nature. Shinrin-yoku or forest bathing essentially proved what Wilson hypothesised: spending time in nature improves health. Blood pressure readings, heart rates and stress levels decrease, and the mind is somewhat relieved from anxiety and depression. Time in nature offers us a new perspective, because the sizes and shapes found in nature are fractals – organised chaos – which pique the mind. And then of course there's the perspective shift of bigness – the trees, the sky, the ocean – and the delight of tiny perfection: the lines of a shell, a delicate cocoon, the vivid blue and orange of forest fungi. Stand on the shore and watch the sea, and you'll find your mind and your thoughts drift with the tides. Because being outside can change the quality of your attention; open space and wild landscape can contour your mood. It's easy to sentimentalise it, to assume that meadows and rivers are only for romantics. But the science supports what our bodies have always told us: bask in nature – or even look at it through a window – and your body responds by restoring what's off kilter, by healing what needs to be repaired.

Since then, hundreds of studies have followed and they all support the fact that being in nature is a positive choice. Even a short walk in a city park can affect brain structure, which creates a sense of calm and results in sharper, productive, creative minds.

Walking, gardening, block building, stirring dinner on the stovetop, needle and thread … When your mind can focus on these things, it has space to untangle sentences and make plot connections, because physical attention alleviates mental distraction, and in the space there's room for sentences to form, plot problems to untangle, answers to lingering questions to appear. And it's not prescriptive either – there are no rules about how many rows you have to knit before you can rush back to the desk with the fluttery potential of a new idea. It's about having the awareness to step away from the work and do something with your body and your hands – anything! It's about learning the beauty and benefit of the practice and knowing that it's helpful. And it's hard, mostly because when time allows we are grasping to be productive and we equate productivity with blatant progress – bums on seats, eyes on screens, a tangible sense of completion by the end of the day. Doing anything with your hands, away from the desk, is easily categorised as 'wasting time', but we don't often think about using our hands (and a very different part of our brain) for opening and freeing the mental pathways required to think, analyse, critique and create – for productivity.

Getting out of your brain and into your body creates space in your mind.

THE VALUE OF ANCIENT PRACTICE

Koren Helbig works in digital technology. Updates and advancements are constant, as is the need to learn them. It's why she finds so much reprieve in her garden, where the skills she learns are ancient and unchanging. 'I work in digital marketing, a tech-based role, so things move at lightning speed,' she says. 'Something I learnt last year may be entirely different this year, so I have to relearn it all and it's taxing on my nervous system. I love the challenge, but it's also a constant pressure.

'In the garden, it's totally different. I've been learning to grow garlic over the past four years. The first year was an abysmal failure; and then I read a how-to and realised I'd done it all wrong. The second year was a big improvement. It's an iterative process that happens over a season or two, and the chance to learn is slowed right down. But when I do learn something, that knowledge is there then – what I learn in year two of growing garlic will apply to the third, fourth, fifth and tenth year of growing garlic. That's not a skill that will change, so there's something really beautiful about old-world, physical, hands-on skills and the way they don't change, and the calming effect they have on me and my world view. It's the opposite of the tech world.'

I don't think it's an exaggeration to say it's the opposite of the whole world. On Westray, one of the northernmost Orkney Islands in Scotland, writer Rebecca Hooper stands on a rock above the 'great lung of ocean' that pulls the pebbles from beneath her and rearranges them with each wave. This island she calls home is tiny – 15 kilometres (9 miles) long, a few miles wide and with a population of around 500 people. Everyone who lives there does so because they have learnt, or are willing to learn, the ancient practice of marking time by bird migrations, whale sightings and weather fronts.

She shares her small house with her partner and their rescue dog. They landed on Westray after she decided to leave the high-pressure work of academia, opting instead for a new way of living: less stress, more space. To reach this windswept corner of the world, Rebecca takes two different boats, island-hopping from the mainland. This journey – of sea and sky – feels to her like an exhalation. 'It's a journey that hands me space, tells me to take it,' she says. 'Being on an island accentuates that feeling because you're forced to be in a small place and know every small thing, and the natural world is in charge here – there's no fighting it or wishing it was another way. You're at the whim of the wind and the storms.'

Rebecca has spent most of her adult life working as a scientist in the lab and in the field, where she would track and observe land and sea creatures. This work is also an art: of sitting in stillness, watching and waiting, but as both Alex and Koren have explained, it is this quiet not-doing that provides inspiration, groundedness and clarity. Sometimes we find it in our normal life, sometimes we shed what no longer feels right and true and choose to step into the not-knowing.

Rebecca admits she was worried that she had romanticised island life. Now, a few years on, she reveres the lessons the land, sea and sky have taught her – mostly the awe that exists when you notice the tiny changes in your own small habitat.

'Getting to know one place intimately is a beautiful thing because there are hundreds of changes every day – geography and the wildlife and the seasons and the rhythm of time. When the geese migrate from Iceland I know autumn is coming, and when the birds start getting territorial about their nest sites you know spring is around the corner. Beautiful little subtle changes, and I find that so rooting, like I belong somewhere, that I'm part of a much bigger web of things and I know my place in it, rather than just being peripheral.'

It's this realisation, and the subsequent respect for the ancient practice of observing and connecting to the natural world, that has helped Rebecca find space in her mind, which has always gone at a million miles an hour, an experience that has been intensely and exhaustingly internal. 'I haven't naturally been someone who pays attention easily, which I now know is because I'm neurodivergent. And I thought at the beginning that I was idealising the feeling of freedom and stillness from when I first visited the island, but the opposite is true. The longer I live here, the more I'm able to find space and stillness in nature. I lose myself in it, my mind slows down. When I pay attention to the external, there is a clarity – a lovely breathing space – in my mind.'

FIVE WAYS TO …
Prioritise creativity

1. Know your best hours. Every cell in your body has a clock, and the master clock is in your brain. Essentially this means that your brain works differently depending on the time of day (this is why we all have particular times when we can predict our brain is going to work more efficiently). This is game-changing for your creativity and productivity because it encourages you to put a firm boundary around the hours when your brain is clear and the work is more likely to flow. This awareness – recognising it, nurturing it – prompts a very real deepening of your creative practice because you're learning *how* you create, not just *what* you create.

2. Value the minutes. We may long for stretches of time to create uninterrupted, but that often doesn't happen in normal life. Instead, revere the small pockets of time that exist between everything else. As writer and mother Kerri ní Dochartaigh says: 'I have found such solace in ritual. In finding ways to hold these minutes, to remind me that they are sacred; they are enough. A candle lit, a hot drink, my favourite pen.'

3. Protect 30 minutes each week to create and don't aim for perfection. Just make your messy, not-quite-right art and do it for yourself because it tends to the deepest, truest part of you.

4. Schedule what you most want. If you find that you never have time to read, write, garden or craft, schedule it in. When you wait for free time to do what really matters to you, you're putting yourself at the end of this list.

5. Accept fear and doubt as a normal part of any creative process and then move on with the creating and making, aware of the fact that a 'fake it till you make it' level of optimism will benefit your creative state.

Conclusion

A new normal is also a joyful beginning; you start to move at your own pace, regardless of where you are in the world.

Psychologists refer to openness as a personality trait, a tendency to seek out and find joy in new, unfamiliar things, which satisfies the reward centre in our brain. When we make small changes to our days, we create this space for ourselves. Stepping into open space fosters our curiosity, boosts our creativity and can slow ageing and our sense of time. Open space doesn't have to be a vast landscape, just like breathing space doesn't require an abundance of time.

We all, at some stage, want to find space – to breathe but also to grieve or process or contemplate, to make decisions or to change course. Creating breathing space is a process of clarity through subtraction, mostly. Sometimes we make big changes and take trusting steps through the in-between; at other times it's about controlling what we can, which may be as simple as the contents of our cupboards.

We can all look at our diaries and exclaim, How are the months passing by so quickly?!, but what we know about time and space is that we do have some control over them if we are aware and attentive. As you're almost ready to close this book and create a new normal for yourself, it's helpful to remember that we will always need to remind ourselves of the benefits of slow work, of quietly noticing, of sitting in space and learning to be okay with what is.

We can come into stillness and quiet and know that it's enough. We don't need to label it self-improvement or self-care. We don't need to apply effort. It can just be what it is – usually imperfect, most likely ordinary, often most easily found at the beginning or end of the day when the light is soft and the world is, too. Here, without any distractions, it is quiet and there is, in tiny glimpses, possibility.

It's not an indulgence to sit with yourself, to check in with your breath and perhaps send it a little deeper, slowing your mind and yourself to notice what arises. Nurturing this intimate knowing of self and place – the topography of your life – regardless of how often and how drastically it changes, allows you to hold stillness wherever you are and wherever you go. There's a shedding of what 'should' be and a sweet acceptance of what is.

When we carve out mellow states in our days – for pottering, pondering, closing our eyes or letting our attention move gently from sky to tree to leaf to ground – we must protect them because the whole world will try to tear us away.

This idea, of being at the whim of the world feels apt at this moment in time, where there is so much uncertainty and so little stability. We all need a safe haven where our brain can breathe, so that space isn't something we chase but something we live with, something we settle into when life feels particularly tempestuous. Author Annie Dillard considers habits a net for catching days, but I think of them more as a lighthouse: steadfast when we feel most untethered, always guiding us back to ourselves.

epilogue

Writing this book prompted me to look for space in my days.
It was there, in all the places I presumed it would be, just waiting
for me to pay attention.

The more I learnt, the more I realised how life-changing this
simple project could be for me. I started to notice the gaps and
carve them out, too. And then I protected them from being
hijacked by whatever else got in the way. I chose space over
doing. I could measure it, too, because if I didn't have space
for a walk on the beach or a focused conversation with a child,
lighting candles on the dinner table or reading a story before
bed, then my day was too full. If there was the option to sit at
my desk wrestling with words that weren't working or walk on
the beach, I'd choose to walk. I got better at work, too. I became
more efficient, I was acutely aware of distractions, and I began
to spend less time on socials. It's been a year-long search for
breathing space – not an arduous hunt, but a slow noticing.
It's changed how I live and I didn't expect that.

Along the way, I've visualised my life as a calendar that
extends over decades and I've looked for all the white space
on the page. It made me think about life as a visual – a series
of days over years – and the feeling of knowing that there are

regular gaps between the doing. I've learnt how to reinstate breathing space in my life: long walks with the dog, slow hours in the garden, afternoon naps, summers off socials, and whole days with no plans. All of these things happen amid the chaos and the humdrum. This is what makes a life.

I keep asking myself: *What is enough?* And this simple question often provides very clear answers. This is a rare experience in a world as complex as ours, but it has allowed me to compartmentalise doing and being, work and rest, clarity and distraction, attention and fascination.

Throughout this process, my work life changed and so too did my income. With less money and more space, I shifted my priorities again. Perhaps it's what comes with age or maybe awareness, but right now I have a deep appreciation for the practical: a garden hose that winds back without struggle, a cotton string bag that stretches to carry all the fruit and veg, shoes that are never not comfortable, an efficient vegetable peeler.

I still admire and revere beautiful things: the beeswax candles on the table that emit a subtle honey scent when lit, the perfect button-up linen shirt, a stack of books fresh from the store that will be cherished for their stories and admired on a shelf.

It's this coexistence of practicality and beauty that means I'm not longing for what I don't have. This wasn't a quick-fix solution to consumerism (and a tendency to be lured by lovely things and whittle away my savings), but I think it's the natural consequence of thoughtful work – considering simplicity and thriftiness and living within my means; thinking deeply about what matters and what doesn't; and, in doing so, learning who I am. It's calculating the cost of things and the time I spend working to buy them, practising patience and using what I have. It's sitting with the disappointment when I make a rash decision, and at times making choices on a whim because nothing in life is static.

I've come to realise that a good life is one in which there's room to move, space to breathe, the opportunity to take a nap. I'd rather earn less and grow a vegetable garden than double my income and navigate persistent exhaustion. Enoughness is a small life and a brain that has the space to breathe no matter the season.

When I was in early pregnancy with my first child, I sat opposite a counsellor who, with her carefully chosen, gentle words and stillness, helped me make sense of the new path I was on. She listened with grace and kindness. 'I had plans to travel to India,' I told her. 'I want to study yoga, to explore spirituality.' She smiled at me. 'You don't need to go anywhere to learn about the spirit; it's within you.'

I was 22 at the time, and while that sentence now seems immature, it was profound enough to stay with me for another 20 years. We all have questions, but we're not very good at waiting for the answers.

This is what I've learnt about breathing space: it's within me, just like it's within you. It is innate human nature to take a breather, to come back to centre and restore our mental and physiological equilibrium with rest. We are creatures who flow; we are, after all, made mostly of water, we were created across billions of years from the dust of stars. We are tiny specks in the universe – thinking, loving, creative humans who thrive when we breathe deeply and fully. And yet the world is pushing this softness out of us, requiring us to be strong and resilient so we can withstand the barrage of information and expectation that follows us around.

If you've ever experienced a period of profound stress, when the acuteness of life impacts your whole being, you'll know the relief of reaching the other side, of feeling like you can finally breathe again. Perhaps you feel as if you're stuck in a fixed state, where your intentions have calcified and you don't seem to have room to move. Breath is a reminder to keep moving, because even small steps towards breathing space are an evolution (perhaps even a revolution).

The truth is that writing this book, making this book from all the parts – research, reading, interviews and curiosity – helped me as a person and also as a writer. You can't write about breathing space and not focus on your breath, you can't learn about your basic biology and not reinstate the habits that nurture it, you can't revere your inner creativity and not respect the rest and quiet your brain needs. As my teacher, author Charlotte Wood says, 'when you're bereft at the state of the world, turning to art can be the reprieve and the hope that you need'. It may not have all the answers, but it gives you a little time, and a welcome perspective shift … the breathing space you need to carry on.

references

Introduction

page 7 *He admits that if we don't give our brain time …*: Supernova, 'How the invention of infinite scrolling turned millions to addiction', Medium, 17 November 2020, medium.com/design-bootcamp/how-the-invention-of-infinite-scrolling-turned-millions-to-addiction-3096602ef9af.

PART ONE: WHAT DO WE REALLY NEED TO LIVE WELL?

page 13 *In the world's largest 'Rest Test' survey …*: Claudia Hammond & Gemma Lewis, 'The rest test: preliminary findings from a large-scale international survey on rest', in Felicity Callard, Kimberley Staines & James Wilkes (eds), *The Restless Compendium: Interdisciplinary Investigations of Rest and its Opposites*, Palgrave Macmillan, Basingstoke, 2016, ncbi.nlm.nih.gov/books/NBK453237.

page 13 *In her poem 'Fire', Judy Brown writes …*: 'Breathing space', Judy Sorum Brown (blog), 15 November 2015, judysorumbrown.com/blog/breathing-space.

page 14 *Poet Naomi Shihab Nye calls this …*: 'Naomi Shihab Nye: "Before you know kindness as the deepest thing inside …"', *On Being with Krista Tippett* (podcast), 28 July 2016, onbeing.org/programs/naomi-shihab-nye-before-you-know-kindness-as-the-deepest-thing-inside.

page 15 *Research shows that the brain – more specifically the hippocampus …*: Alexandra De Soares, Tony Kim, Franck Mugisho et al., 'Top-down attention shifts behavioral and neural event boundaries in narratives with overlapping event scripts', *Current Biology*, 2024, vol. 34, no. 20, pp. 4729–42.E5, doi.org/10.1016/j.cub.2024.09.013.

page 17 *For a doctor it's altering one person's experience …*: Stephen Trzeciak & Anthony Mazzarelli, *Compassionomics: The Revolutionary Scientific Evidence that Caring Makes a Difference*, Studer Group, Pensacola, Florida, 2019.

page 17 *Writer Annie Dillard refers to habits …*: Annie Dillard, *The Writing Life*, Harper & Row, New York, 1989.

page 18 *Haruki Murakami refers to these tiny morsels …*: Haruki Murakami, 'Afternoon in the Islets of Langerhans', 新潮文庫 (Shincho bunko), Tokyo, 1990.

1. A calm nervous system

page 22 *Generalised unsafety is also an evolutionary survival mechanism …*: Jos F. Brosschot, Bart Verkuil & Julian F. Thayer, 'Exposed to events that never happen: generalized unsafety, the default stress response, and prolonged autonomic activity', *Neuroscience & Biobehavioral Reviews*, 2017, vol. 74, Part B, pp. 287–96, doi.org/10.1016/j.neubiorev.2016.07.019.

page 22 *loneliness – now a public health concern with a physical impact equivalent to smoking 15 cigarettes a day*: 'WHO Commission on Social Connection', World Health Organization, who.int/groups/commission-on-social-connection; US Surgeon General, *Our Epidemic of Loneliness and Isolation: US Surgeon General's Advisory on the Healing Effects of Social Connection and Community*, Office of the US Surgeon General, Washington, DC, 2023, hhs.gov/sites/default/files/surgeon-general-social-connection-advisory.pdf.

page 22 *And yet as renowned Buddhist teacher Pema Chödrön says …*: Pema Chödrön, *Comfortable with Uncertainty: 108 Teachings on Cultivating Fearlessness and Compassion*, Shambhala, Boston, Massachusetts, 2002.

page 23 *The way we perceive stress also determines …*: Victoria M. Indivero, 'Let it go: reaction to stress more important than its frequency', PennState, 25 February 2016, psu.edu/news/research/story/let-it-go-reaction-stress-more-important-its-frequency.

page 26 *High cortisol is also associated with an increase in negative thinking and lower quality of life …*: Susan Jennifer Thomas & Theresa Larkin, 'Cognitive distortions in relation to plasma cortisol and oxytocin levels in major depressive disorder', *Frontiers in Psychiatry*, 2020, vol. 10, article no. 971, doi.org/10.3389/fpsyt.2019.00971; Ai Ling Tang, Susan J. Thomas & Theresa Larkin, 'Cortisol, oxytocin, and quality of life in major depressive disorder', *Quality of Life Research*, 2019, vol. 28, pp. 2919–28, doi.org/10.1007/s11136-019-02236-3.

page 27 *Cortisol isn't all bad either; it's … vital for survival*: Lauren Thau, Jayashree Gandhi & Sandeep Sharma, 'Physiology, cortisol', StatPearls, 2023, ncbi.nlm.nih.gov/books/NBK538239.

page 27 *when cortisol remains high … it can take weeks for this dysregulation …*: Omer Karin, Moriya Raz, Avichai Tendler et al., 'A new model for the HPA axis explains dysregulation of stress hormones on the timescale of weeks', *Molecular Systems Biology*, 2020, vol. 16, article no. e9510, doi.org/10.15252/msb.20209510.

page 28 *it's also more prevalent in younger adults …*: Australian Bureau of Statistics, 'First insights from the National Study of Mental Health and Wellbeing, 2020–21', 8 December 2021, ABS, abs.gov.au/articles/first-insights-national-study-mental-health-and-wellbeing-2020-21.

page 28 *housing worries and the pressure to succeed predominant concerns*: 'Stress: statistics', 2018, Mental Health Foundation (UK), mentalhealth.org.uk/explore-mental-health/statistics/stress-statistics.

2. An uncluttered brain

page 32 *upwards of 6000 thoughts …*: Julie Tseng & Jordan Poppenk, 'Brain meta-state transitions demarcate thoughts across task contexts exposing the mental noise of trait neuroticism', *Nature Communications*, 2020, vol. 11, article no. 3480, doi.org/10.1038/s41467-020-17255-9.

page 40 *This exact timing is important; it's called the Mayer rhythm …*: Luciano Bernardi, Peter Sleight, Gabriele Bandinelli et al., 'Effect of rosary prayer and yoga mantras on autonomic cardiovascular rhythms: comparative study', *BMJ*, 2001, vol. 323, no. 7327, pp. 1446–49, doi.org/10.1136/bmj.323.7327.1446.

3. A safe, nourished body that moves and rests

page 43 *Despite the fact that in the nineteenth century …*: Jessie Mond Wedd & Frieda Gormley, 'UK dictionary open letter', 2023, We Are Nature, wearenature.org/open-letter.

page 45 *As author Sinéad Gleeson says …*: Sinéad Gleeson, *Constellations: Reflections from Life*, Picador, London, 2019.

4. Breathing space

page 52 *In her second book,* An Experiment in Leisure *…*: Marion Milner, *An Experiment in Leisure*, Virago, London, 1986, p. 221 (first published by Chatto & Windus, London, 1937).

page 55 *A recent study on mental wellbeing says …*: D.M. Ferraro, Z.D. Miller, L.A. Ferguson et al., 'The phantom chorus: birdsong boosts human well-being in protected areas', *Proceedings of the Royal Society B: Biological Sciences*, 2020, vol. 287, no. 1941, article no. 20201811, doi.org/10.1098/rspb.2020.1811.

page 56 *Jamaican novelist and screenwriter Sara Collins …*: Sara Collins, Sharmaine Lovegrove & Nelle Andrew, *How to Write a Book* (podcast), podcasts.apple.com/au/podcast/how-to-write-a-book/id1806164300.

page 59 *In 2019 the World Health Organization …*: 'Burn-out an "occupational phenomenon"': 'International Classification of Diseases', WHO, 28 May 2019, who.int/news/item/28-05-2019-burn-out-an-occupational-phenomenon-international-classification-of-diseases.

page 61 *busyness is a modern measure of social status …*: Jonathan Gershuny, 'Busyness as the badge of honor for the new superordinate working class', *Social Research*, 2005, vol. 72, no. 2, pp. 287–314, jstor.org/stable/40971766.

page 62 *This is particularly apt for people with higher acute sensory processing sensitivity …*: Krystyna Golonka & Bozena Gulla, 'Individual differences and susceptibility to burnout syndrome: sensory processing sensitivity and its relation to exhaustion and disengagement', *Frontiers in Psychology*, 2021, vol. 12, article no. 751350, doi.org/10.3389/fpsyg.2021.751350.

page 64 *New research suggests that burnout isn't solely dictated …*: Jonathan Gershuny, 'Busyness as the badge of honor for the new superordinate working class', *Social Research*, 2005, vol. 72, no. 2, pp. 287–314, jstor.org/stable/40971766.

page 64 *For many autistic people …*: Jane Mantzalas, Amanda L. Richdale, Achini Adikari et al., 'What is autistic burnout? a thematic analysis of posts on two online platforms', *Autism in Adulthood*, 2022, vol. 4, no. 1, pp. 52–65, doi.org/10.1089/aut.2021.0021.

page 64 *One study of 42 countries shows that the highest prevalence rates …*: Isabelle Roskam, Joyce Aguiar, Ege Akgun et al., 'Parental burnout around the globe: a 42-country study', *Affective Science*, 2021, vol. 2, pp. 58–79, doi.org/10.1007/s42761-020-00028-4.

page 65 *what's known as the woman's 'fourth shift' …*: Susan Venn, Sara Arber, Robert Meadows & Jenny Hislop, 'The fourth shift: exploring the gendered nature of sleep disruption among couples with children', *British Journal of Sociology*, 2008, vol. 59, no. 1, pp. 79–97, doi.org/10.1111/j.1468-4446.2007.00183.x.

page 66 *This space is beneficial for children, too*: Florida Atlantic University, '"All work, no independent play" cause of children's declining mental health', ScienceDaily, 9 March 2023, sciencedaily.com/releases/2023/03/230309101330.htm.

page 68 *Studies show that when new parents leave the house …*: Katherine Hall, Jonathan Evans, Rosa Roberts et al., 'Mothers' accounts of the impact of being in nature on postnatal wellbeing: a focus group study', *BMC Women's Health*, 2023, vol. 23, article no. 32, doi.org/10.1186/s12905-023-02165-x.

page 67 *In her 2019 survey 'The Rest Test …*: Claudia Hammond & Gemma Lewis, 'The rest test: preliminary findings from a large-scale international survey on rest', in Felicity Callard, Kimberley Staines & James Wilkes (eds), *The Restless Compendium: Interdisciplinary Investigations of Rest and its Opposites*, Palgrave Macmillan, Basingstoke, 2016, ncbi.nlm.nih.gov/books/NBK453237.

PART TWO: HOW TO CREATE YOUR NEW NORMAL

pages 72–73 *Research shows that the part of the brain that senses danger …*: Florian Lederbogen, Peter Kirsch, Leila Haddad et al., 'City living and urban upbringing affect neural social stress processing in humans', *Nature*, 2011, vol. 474, pp. 498–501, doi.org/10.1038/nature10190.

page 73 *studies support the protective effects of exposure to nature …*: Marcia P. Jimenez, Nicole V. DeVille, Elise G. Elliott et al., 'Associations between nature exposure and health: a review of the evidence', *International Journal of Environmental Research and Public Health*, 2021, vol. 18, no. 9, article no. 4790 doi.org/10.3390/ijerph18094790.

page 73 *Experiencing small parcels of nature … hearing birdsong*: Marcia P. Jimenez, Nicole V. DeVille, Elise G. Elliott et al., 'Associations between nature exposure and health: a review of the evidence', *International Journal of Environmental Research and Public Health*, 2021, vol. 18, no. 9, article no. 4790 doi.org/10.3390/ijerph18094790.

page 74 *And it's this ease – what some refer to as mindfulness*: Zoe Hughes, Linden J. Ball, Cassandra Richardson & Jeannie Judge, 'A meta-analytical review of the impact of mindfulness on creativity: framing current lines of research and defining moderator variables', *Psychonomic Bulletin and Review*, 2023, vol. 30, no. 6, pp. 2155–86, doi.org/10.3758/s13423-023-02327-w.

page 74 *that has been proven to benefit creativity and productivity*: Matthijs Baas, Carsten K.W. De Dreu & Bernard A. Nijstad. 'A meta-analysis of 25 years of mood-creativity research: hedonic tone, activation, or regulatory focus?', *Psychological Bulletin*, vol. 134, no. 6, pp. 779–806, doi.org/10.1037/a0012815.

1. Pay attention to the gaps

page 78 *Attention, says David Foster Wallace in his essay …*: David Foster Wallace, *This Is Water*, Little, Brown, New York, 2009.

page 83 *what author Elizabeth Strout refers to …*: Barbara DeMarco-Barrett & Marrie Stone, 'Elizabeth Strout, author of *Tell Me Everything*', *Writers on Writing* (podcast), 9 September 2024, open.spotify.com/episode/4GSi2MhJp3hN83mynXSM4b.

2. Befriend your vagus nerve

page 88 *A well-trained vagus nerve is said to have high vagal tone*: Julian F. Thayer, Anira L. Hansen, Evelyn Saus-Rose & Bjorn H. Johnsen, 'Heart rate variability, prefrontal neural function, and cognitive performance: the neurovisceral integration perspective on self-regulation, adaptation, and health', *Annals of Behavioral Medicine*, 2009, vol. 37, pp. 141–53, doi.org/10.1007/s12160-009-9101-z.

page 89 *Research confirms the profound connection between body and mind* ...: Sigrid Breit, Aleksandra Kupferberg, Gerhard Rogler & Gregor Hasler, 'Vagus nerve as modulator of the brain–gut axis in psychiatric and inflammatory disorders', *Frontiers in Psychiatry*, 2018, vol. 9, article no. 44, doi.org/10.3389/fpsyt.2018.00044.

page 90 *Research shows that men and women respond differently* ...: Kasiphak Kaikaew, Johanna C. van den Beukel, Sebastian Neggers et al., 'Sex difference in cold perception and shivering onset upon gradual cold exposure', *Journal of Thermal Biology*, 2018, vol. 77, pp. 137–44, doi.org/10.1016/j.jtherbio.2018.08.016.

page 90 *However, a recent study on cold-water swimming* ...: Megan Pound, Heather Massey, Sasha Roseneil et al., 'How do women feel cold water swimming affects their menstrual and perimenopausal symptoms?', *Post Reproductive Health*, 2024, vol. 30, no. 1, pp. 11–27, doi.org/10.1177/20533691241227100.

page 90 *Diaphragmatic breathing ... is proven to increase comfort, relaxation and alertness* ...: Andrea Zaccaro, Andrea Piarulli, Marco Laurino et al., 'How breath-control can change your life: a systematic review on psycho-physiological correlates of slow breathing', *Frontiers in Human Neuroscience*, 2018, vol. 12, article no. 353, doi.org/10.3389/fnhum.2018.00353.

page 90 *It's best practised in a supine position*: Swami Rama, Rudolph Ballentine & Alan Hymes, *Science of Breath: A Practical Guide*, Himalayan Institute Press, Honesdale, Pennsylvania, 1998, pp. 26–44.

page 91 *studies show that head and neck massage can stimulate the vagus nerve* ...: Maria Meier, Eva Unternaehrer, Stephanie J. Dimitroff et al., 'Standardized massage interventions as protocols for the induction of psychophysiological relaxation in the laboratory: a block randomized, controlled trial', *Scientific Reports*, 2020, vol. 10, no. 1, article no. 14774, doi.org/10.1038/s41598-020-71173-w.

3. Find your best forms of rest

page 93 *Rest ... subjective, vaguely defined*: Esther I. Bernhofer, 'Investigating the concept of rest for research and practice', *Journal of Advanced Nursing*, 2016, vol. 72, no. 5, pp. 1012–22.

page 95 *Their scientific study supports what humans intuitively know* ...: Alexandra D. Crosswell, Stefanie E. Mayer, Lauren N. Whitehurst et al., 'Deep rest: an integrative model of how contemplative practices combat stress and enhance the body's restorative capacity', *Psychological Review*, 2024, vol. 131, no. 1, pp. 247–70, doi.org/10.1037/rev0000453.

page 96 *slow breathing changes our physiology and our mood*: Marc A. Russo, Danielle M. Santarelli & Dean O'Rourke, 'The physiological effects of slow breathing in the healthy human', *Breathe* (Sheffield), 2017, vol. 13, no. 4, pp. 298–309, doi.org/10.1183/20734735.009817.

page 97 *Some health studies suggest that burnout …*: Anita Eskildsen, Lars P. Andersen, Anders D. Pedersen & Johan H. Andersen, 'Cognitive impairments in former patients with work-related stress complaints – one year later', *Stress*, 2016, vol. 19, no. 6, pp. 559–66, doi.org/10.1080/10253890.2016.1222370.

page 97 *One scientific literature review shows that 25–50 per cent …*: Arno van Dam, 'A clinical perspective on burnout: diagnosis, classification, and treatment of clinical burnout', *European Journal of Work and Organizational Psychology*, 2021, vol. 30, no. 5, pp. 732–41, doi.org/10.1080/1359432X.2021.1948400.

page 100 *Yoga nidra … some sources claim that the 30–60-minute practice …*: Kamakhya Kumar, *A Handbook of Yoga-Nidra*, D.K. Printworld, New Delhi, 2013, p. 260.

page 100 *The positive effects on the central nervous system …*: Seithikurippu R. Pandi-Perumal, David Warren Spence, Neena Srivastava, et al., 'The origin and clinical relevance of yoga nidra', *Sleep and Vigilance*, 2022, vol. 6, no. 1, pp. 61–84, doi.org/10.1007/s41782-022-00202-7.

page 100 *some sources refer to it as a 'third mental state'*: Seithikurippu R. Pandi-Perumal, David Warren Spence, Neena Srivastava, et al., 'The origin and clinical relevance of yoga nidra', *Sleep and Vigilance*, 2022, vol. 6, no. 1, pp. 61–84, doi.org/10.1007/s41782-022-00202-7.

4. Honour the season you're in

page 104 *Nearly every tissue and organ within the body has its own circadian rhythm …*: 'Circadian rhythms', 2023, National Institute of General Medical Research (US), nigms.nih.gov/education/fact-sheets/Pages/circadian-rhythms.

page 111 *In her 1937 book* An Experiment in Leisure *…*: Marion Milner, *An Experiment in Leisure*, Virago, London, 1986, p. 221 (first published by Chatto & Windus, London, 1937).

page 111 *And while the transition from foraging to farming …*: Mark Dyble, Jack Thorley, Abigail E. Page et al., 'Engagement in agricultural work is associated with reduced leisure time among Agta hunter-gatherers', *Nature Human Behaviour*, 2019, vol. 3, pp. 792–796, doi.org/10.1038/s41562-019-0614-6.

page 115 *Hope, Rebecca Solnit writes …*: Rebecca Solnit, '"Hope is an embrace of the unknown"': 'Rebecca Solnit on living in dark times', *The Guardian*, 15 July 2016, theguardian.com/books/2016/jul/15/rebecca-solnit-hope-in-the-dark-new-essay-embrace-unknown.

5. Slow down and sidestep

page 120 *Women are more likely to experience sleep disturbances …*: Eva Lindberg, Christer Janson, Thorarinn Gislason et al., 'Sleep disturbances in a young adult population: can gender differences be explained by differences in psychological status?', *Sleep*, 1997, vol. 20, no. 6, pp. 381–87, doi.org/10.1093/sleep/20.6.381.

page 121 *there's also research that points to the ancient practice of 'two sleeps'*: Niall Boyce, 'Have we lost sleep? A reconsideration of segmented sleep in early modern England', *Medical History*, 2023, vol. 67, no. 2, pp. 91–108, doi.org/10.1017/mdh.2023.14.

page 122 *Professor Russell Foster … reiterates on the* Just One Thing *podcast …*: 'Sleep special – with Prof Russell Foster', *Just One Thing – with Michael Mosley* (podcast), BBC, bbc.co.uk/sounds/play/m001trnj.

page 124 *a 2009 study showed that reading for six minutes …*: David Lewis, 'Galaxy stress research', Mindlab International, Sussex University, Brighton, 2009.

page 125 *Researchers at Yale University's School of Public Health …*: Avni Bavishi, Martin D. Slade & Becca R. Levy, 'A chapter a day: association of book reading with longevity', *Social Science and Medicine*, 2016, vol. 164, pp 44–48, doi.org/10.1016/j.socscimed.2016.07.014

page 125 *A recent study by the Queen's Reading Room …*: 'The Queen's Reading Room study', The Queen's Reading Room, 2023, thequeensreadingroom.co.uk/the-queens-reading-room-study.

page 127 *I may be romanticising … decreases anxiety, rumination and emotional reactivity*: Lingyun Mao, Pan Li, Yunhong Wu, Lan Luo & Maorong Hu, 'The effectiveness of mindfulness-based interventions for ruminative thinking: a systematic review and meta-analysis of randomized controlled trials', *Journal of Affective Disorders*, 2023, vol. 321, pp. 83–95, doi.org/10.1016/j.jad.2022.10.022.

6. Check your habits

page 130 *It's composed of approximately 100 billion neurons*: Suzana Herculano-Houzel, 'The human brain in numbers: a linearly scaled-up primate brain', *Frontiers in Human Neuroscience*, 2009, vol. 3, article no. 31, doi.org/10.3389/neuro.09.031.2009.

page 130 *carry information travelling up to 430 kilometres (270 miles) per hour*: R. Káradóttir & D. Attwell, 'Neurotransmitter receptors in the life and death of oligodendrocytes', *Neuroscience*, 2007, vol. 145, no. 4, pp. 1426–38, doi.org/10.1016/j.neuroscience.2006.08.070.

page 130 *The brain uses 20 per cent of all the energy …*: Marcus E. Raichle & Debra A. Gusnard, 'Appraising the brain's energy budget', *Proceedings of the National Academy of Sciences of the United States*, 2002, vol. 99, no. 16, pp. 10237–39, doi.org/10.1073/pnas.172399499.

pages 130–33 *Dr Gina Cleo, who is at the forefront … As Cleo explains in her book …*: Gina Cleo, *The Habit Revolution: Simple Steps to Rewire Your Brain for Powerful Habit Change*, Murdoch Books, Sydney, 2024.

page 133 *US psychiatrist Dr Anna Lembke refers …*: 'Digital drugs have us hooked: Dr. Anna Lembke Sees a Way Out', The Interview, New York Times, 1 February 2025, youtube.com/watch?v=j46DvZy4vdg.

page 133 *'Is this how you want to spend your life?' …*: August Lamm, *You Don't Need a Smartphone: A Practical Guide to Downgrading and Reclaiming Your Life*, self-published pamphlet, 2024, augustlamm.com/shop/you-dont-need-a-smartphone-digital.

page 134 *But as one study of people who reported high levels …*: Chiara Samele, Harry Lees-Manning, Victoria Zamperoni et al., *Stress: Are We Coping?*, Mental Health Foundation, London, 2018, p. 16, mentalhealth.org.uk/sites/default/files/2022-08/stress-are-we-coping.pdf.

page 137 *The Oxford English Dictionary's 2024 'word' of the year …*: '"Brain rot" named Oxford Word of the Year 2024', Oxford University Press, 2 December 2024, corp.oup.com/news/brain-rot-named-oxford-word-of-the-year-2024.

page 137 *while psychologists say that consuming digital content …*: '"Brain rot" and digital overload: more myth than menace', UNSW Sydney Newsroom, 7 November 2024, unsw.edu.au/newsroom/news/2024/10/brain-rot-more-myth-menace.

page 137 *Studies show that on average, we spend a mere 40 seconds viewing something on a screen …*: Gloria Mark, *Attention Span: Finding Focus for a Fulfilling Life*, William Collins, London, 2023.

page 137 *Novelist and playwright Saul Bellow …*: Gloria L. Cronin & Ben Siegel (eds), *Conversations with Saul Bellow*, University Press of Mississippi, Jackson, 1995, p. 70.

page 137 *Research shows that mindful breathing …*: Laura G. Kiken & Natalie J. Shook, 'Looking up: mindfulness increases positive judgments and reduces negativity bias', *Social Psychological and Personality Science*, 2011, vol. 2, no. 4, pp. 425–31, doi.org/10.1177/1948550610396585.

page 138 *But it's actually a non-existent cognitive skill – the human brain is incapable …*: Paul Atchley, 'You can't multitask, so stop trying', *Harvard Business Review*, 22 December 2010, hbr.org/2010/12/you-cant-multi-task-so-stop-tr.

page 138 *It even has a name: 'the switch cost effect'*: Glenn Wylie & Alan Allport, 'Task switching and the measurement of "switch costs"', *Psychological Research*, 2000, vol. 63, nos 3–4, pp. 212–33, doi.org/10.1007/s004269900003.

page 139 *This is reflected in the statistic that the unpaid care industry …*: Workplace Gender Equality Agency, *Unpaid Care Work and the Labour Market: Insight Paper*, Australian Government, Canberra, 2016, wgea.gov.au/sites/default/files/documents/australian-unpaid-care-work-and-the-labour-market.pdf.

7. Savour the good

page 143 *The memories we form through these experiences …*: Elizabeth A. Kensinger, 'Remembering the details: effects of emotion', *Emotion Review*, 2009, vol. 1, no. 2, pp. 99–113, doi.org/10.1177/1754073908100432.

page 144 *'Find the time and space to do the things that you're going to remember'*: Miriam Frankel, 'Does life feel like it's speeding up? How to slow down time in 2025', *The Guardian*, 29 December 2024, theguardian.com/science/2024/dec/29/does-life-feel-like-its-speeding-up-how-to-slow-down-time-in-2025.

page 144 *Dr Marc Wittmann from the Institute for Frontier Areas of Psycholgy and Mental Health …*: Marc Wittmann, Simone Otten, Eva Schötz et al., 'Subjective expansion of extended time-spans in experienced meditators', *Frontiers in Psychology*, 2015, vol. 5, article no. 1586, doi.org/10.3389/fpsyg.2014.01586.

pages 144–45 *Behavioural economist Dr Sendhil Mullainathan …*: by Sendhil Mullainathan & Eldar Shafir, *Scarcity: The True Cost of Not Having Enough*, Penguin, London, 2014.

page 145 *Dr Anna Lembke refers to this as the 'plenty paradox'*: 'Digital drugs have us hooked. Dr Anna Lembke sees a way out', *New York Times*, 1 February 2025, nytimes.com/2025/02/01/magazine/anna-lembke-interview.html.

page 145 *Studies show that simply being attentive to life …*: Marc Wittmann, Simone Otten, Eva Schötz et al., 'Subjective expansion of extended time-spans in experienced meditators', *Frontiers in Psychology*, 2015, vol. 5, article no. 1586, doi.org/10.3389/fpsyg.2014.01586.

page 147 *Research shows that this negativity bias …*: Amrisha Vaish, Tobias Grossmann & Amanda Woodward, 'Not all emotions are created equal: the negativity bias in social-emotional development', *Psychological Bulletin*, 2008, vol. 134, no. 3, pp. 383–403, doi.org/10.1037/0033-2909.134.3.383.

page 148 *This is one part of the Savoring Beliefs Inventory …*: Fred Bryant, 'Savoring Beliefs Inventory (SBI): a scale for measuring beliefs about savouring', *Journal of Mental Health*, 2003, vol. 12, no. 2, pp. 175–96, doi.org/10.1080/0963823031000103489.

page 148 *new research shows that cells in the body can learn and form memories too*: N.V. Kukushkin, R.E. Carney, T. Tabassum et al., 'The massed-spaced learning effect in non-neural human cells', *Nature Communications*, 2024, vol. 15, article no. 9635, doi.org/10.1038/s41467-024-53922-x.

page 148 *Our survival and wellness require a balance of optimism and pessimism …*: David Hecht, 'The neural basis of optimism and pessimism', *Experimental Neurobiology*, 2013, vol. 22, no. 3, pp. 173–99, doi.org/10.5607/en.2013.22.3.173.

page 149 *Journalist Imogen West-Knight refers to it …*: Imogen West-Knight, 'Treat brain: how the pandemic is rewiring our minds', *FT Magazine*, 25 August 2021, ft.com/content/3ed08931-80b0-43a0-9bba-6c4bcc1b3e70.

page 149 *This is dependent on noticing and savouring positive emotions …*: Michelle G. Craske, Alicia E. Meuret, Aileen Echiverri-Cohen et al., 'Positive affect treatment targets reward sensitivity: a randomized controlled trial', *Journal of Consulting and Clinical Psychology*, 2023, vol. 91, no. 6, pp. 350–66, doi.org/10.1037/ccp0000805.

page 151 *Research shows that when we do this …*: Anne Arewasikporn, John A. Sturgeon & Alex J. Zautra, 'Sharing positive experiences boosts resilient thinking: everyday benefits of social connection and positive emotion in a community sample', *Community Psychology*, 2019, vol. 63, nos 1–2, pp. 110–21, doi.org/10.1002/ajcp.12279.

8. Restore your attention

page 158 *There's been a lot of talk about awe in recent years thanks …*: Maria Monroy & Dacher Keltner, 'Awe as a pathway to mental and physical health', *Perspectives on Psychological Science*, 2023, vol. 18, no. 2, pp. 309–20, doi.org/10.1177/17456916221094856.

page 160 *Studies show that when we're in a green space …*: Avik Basu, Jason Duvall & Rachel Kaplan, 'Attention restoration theory: exploring the role of soft fascination and mental bandwidth', *Environment and Behavior*, 2018, vol. 51, nos 9–10, pp. 1055–81, doi.org/10.1177/0013916518774400.

page 160 *there's also a helpful set timeframe … 20 minutes … lowers our cortisol levels*: MaryCarol R. Hunter, Brenda W. Gillespie & Sophie Yu-Pu Chen, 'Urban nature experiences reduce stress in the context of daily life based on salivary biomarkers', *Frontiers in Psychology*, 2019, vol. 10, article no. 722, doi.org/10.3389/fpsyg.2019.00722.

page 167 *Research shows that it reduces activity in the amygdala …*: Matthew D. Lieberman, Naomi I. Eisenberger, Molly J. Crockett et al., 'Putting feelings into words: affect labeling disrupts amygdala activity in response to affective stimuli', *Psychological Science*, 2007, vol. 18, no. 5, pp. 421–28, doi.org/10.1111/j.1467-9280.2007.01916.x.

9. Let your mind wander

page 169 *Most of us 'digitally switch' …*: Katy Y.Y. Tam & Michael Inzlicht, 'Fast-forward to boredom: how switching behavior on digital media makes people more bored', *Journal of Experimental Psychology: General*, 2024, vol. 53, no. 10, pp. 2409–26, doi.org/10.1037/xge0001639.

page 170 *boredom provides unpleasant but important feedback*: Erin Corwin Westgate, 'Why boredom is interesting', PhD thesis, University of Virginia, 2018, osf.io/preprints/thesiscommons/qxh83_v1.

page 170 *research tells us the best path forward is to get a bit bored*: Guihyun Park, Beng-Chong Lim & Hui Si Oh, 'Why being bored might not be a bad thing after all', *Academy of Management Discoveries*, 2019, vol. 5, no. 1, pp. 78–92, doi.org/10.5465/amd.2017.0033.

page 170 *mind-wandering is an exploratory response to boredom …*: Corinna S. Martarelli & Ambroise Baillifard, 'Mind-wandering as an exploratory response to boredom', in Maik Bieleke, Wanja Wolff & Corinna S. Martarelli (eds), *The Routledge International Handbook of Boredom*, Routledge, London, 2024, pp. 145–62.

page 171 *Research suggests that we spend nearly 50 per cent …*: Matthew A. Killingsworth & Daniel T. Gilbert, 'A wandering mind is an unhappy mind', *Science*, 2010, vol. 330, no. 6006, p. 932, doi.org/10.1126/science.1192439.

page 171 *Scientists believe that the wandering mind …*: Matthew A. Killingsworth & Daniel T. Gilbert, 'A wandering mind is an unhappy mind', *Science*, 2010, vol. 330, no. 6006, p. 932, doi.org/10.1126/science.1192439.

page 171 *But more recent research offers slightly more nuance …*: Benjamin Baird, Jonathan Smallwood, Michael D. Mrazek et al., 'Inspired by distraction: mind wandering facilitates creative incubation', *Psychological Science*, 2012, vol. 23, no. 10, pp. 1117–22, doi.org/10.1177/0956797612446024; Jill Suttie, How mind-wandering may be good for you', *Greater Good Magazine*, 14 February 2018, greatergood.berkeley.edu/article/item/how_mind_wandering_may_be_good_for_you.

page 171 *Professor James Danckert says …*: Mike Sowden, 'Why, boredom, why?', Everything Is Amazing, 12 September 2024, everythingisamazing.substack.com/p/why-boredom-why.

page 172 *In 2014, University of Virginia researchers …*: Timothy D. Wilson, David A. Reinhard, Erin C. Westgate et al., 'Just think: the challenges of the disengaged mind', *Science*, 2014, vol. 345, no. 6192, pp. 75–77, doi.org/10.1126/science.1250830.

page 172 *One study found that those who had engaged in a boring task …*: Sandi Mann & Rebekah Cadman, 'Does being bored make us more creative?', *Creativity Research Journal*, 2014, vol. 26, no. 2, pp. 165–73, doi.org/10.1080/10400419.2014.901073.

page 173 *He likened it to happiness …*: Mihaly Csikszentmihalyi, *Flow: The Psychology of Optimal Experience*, Harper & Row, New York, 1990, p. 3.

page 174 *One 10-year longitudinal study showed …*: Susie Cranston & Scott Keller, 'Increasing the "meaning quotient" of work', *McKinsey Quarterly*, 2013, no. 1, pp. 48–59, mckinsey.com/capabilities/people-and-organizational-performance/our-insights/increasing-the-meaning-quotient-of-work.

page 174 *In a flow state, there is decreased activity in the prefrontal cortex …*: Arne Dietrich, 'Neurocognitive mechanisms underlying the experience of flow', *Consciousness and Cognition*, 2004, vol. 13, no. 4, pp. 746–61, doi.org/10.1016/ j.concog.2004.07.002.

page 174 *Flow is associated with the brain's reward circuitry …*: Matthias J. Gruber, Barnard D. Gelman, Charan Ranganath, 'States of curiosity modulate hippocampus-dependent learning via the dopaminergic circuit', *Neuron*, 2014, vol. 84, no. 2, pp. 486–96, doi.org/10.1016/j.neuron.2014.08.060.

page 175 *Csikszentmihalyi said it well …*: Mihaly Csikszentmihalyi, *Flow: The Psychology of Optimal Experience*, Harper & Row, New York, 1990, p. 3.

page 178 *Cognitive insights arrive when the mind dissociates*: Simone Sandkühler & Joydeep Bhattacharya, 'Deconstructing insight: EEG correlates of insightful problem solving', *PLOS One*, 2008, vol. 3, no. 1, article no. e1459, doi.org/10.1371/journal. pone.0001459.

page 182 *44 per cent of young people say they feel stressed …*: 'Mental health and stress top concerns for young Australians', Orygen, 2 December 2021, orygen.org.au/About/ News-And-Events/2021/Mental-health-and-stress-top-concerns-for-young-Au.

page 182 *In a 2023 American Psychological Society survey …*: 'Stress in America 2023: a nation recovering from collective trauma', American Psychological Association, November 2023, apa.org/news/press/releases/stress/2023/collective-trauma-recovery.

10. Walk the in-between

page 186 *In her book* Chasing Fog …: Laura Pashby, *Chasing Fog: Finding Enchantment in a Cloud*, Simon & Schuster, London, 2024.

page 187 *… aligning mind, body and the world …*: Rebecca Solnit, *Wanderlust: A History of Walking*, Granta, London, 2022.

page 188 *Perhaps this is why author and activist Jane Jacobs …*: Jane Jacobs, *The Death and Life of Great American Cities*, Random House, New York, 1961.

page 190 *In her book* A Walking Life, *Antonia Malchik writes …*: Antonia Malchik, *A Walking Life*, Little, Brown, New York, 2019.

page 191 *Engineering researchers look to nature …*: 'Tough, light and strong: lessons from nature could lead to the creation of new materials, science study says', UC San Diego, 14 February 2013, jacobsschool.ucsd.edu/news/release/1312?id=1312.

11. Repair and make space

page 205 *Paul Dolan, author of* Happiness by Design *says* …: Joel Suss, 'Five minutes with Paul Dolan: "Happiness is experiences of pleasure and purpose over time"', LSE blog, 30 August 2014, blogs.lse.ac.uk/europpblog/2014/08/30/five-minutes-with-paul-dolan-happiness-is-experiences-of-pleasure-and-purpose-over-time.

page 209 *As writer and psychologist Andrew Solomon says* …: Andrew Solomon, 'Depression, the secret we share', TEDxMet, October 2013, ted.com/talks/andrew_solomon_depression_the_secret_we_share?language=en.

page 210 *But science also suggests that frugality* …: Joseph Chancellor & Sonja Lyubomirsky, 'Happiness and thrift: When (spending) less is (hedonically) more', *Journal of Consumer Psychology*, 2011, vol. 21, no. 2, pp. 131–38, doi.org/10.1016/j.jcps.2011.02.004.

page 212 *And while we may be chasing perfection* …: Avram Alpert, 'The good-enough life', *New York Times*, 20 February 2019, nytimes.com/2019/02/20/opinion/the-good-enough-life-philosophy.html.

page 213 *American beauty journalist Jessica DeFino coined the term 'sale gaze'*: Jessica DeFino, 'The rise and rise of "dewy dumpling skin"', *The Times*, 8 October 2023, thetimes.com/life-style/beauty/article/the-rise-and-rise-of-dewy-dumpling-skin-v9mwk2qzc.

page 214 *We are primed to look for novelty* …: Adrian J. Duszkiewicz, Colin G. McNamara, Tomonori Takeuchi & Lisa Genzel, 'Novelty and dopaminergic modulation of memory persistence: a tale of two systems', *Trends in Neurosciences*, 2019, vol. 42, no. 2, pp. 102–14, doi.org/10.1016/j.tins.2018.10.002.

page 215 *The French government recognises it as a practical way* …: 'France to pay bonus for shoes and clothing repairs to cut waste', *Le Monde* with AFP, 12 July 2023, lemonde.fr/en/environment/article/2023/07/12/france-to-pay-bonus-for-shoe-clothes-repairs-to-cut-waste_6050031_114.html.

page 216 *Science also tells us* …: Kent C. Berridge & Morten L. Kringelbach, 'Building a neuroscience of pleasure and well-being', *Psychology of Well-Being*, 2011, vol. 1, article no. 3, doi.org/10.1186/2211-1522-1-3.

page 222 *It reminds me of Anne Morrow* …: Anne Morrow Lindbergh, *Gift from the Sea*, Pantheon Books, New York, 1955.

12. Build space to create

page 229 *Australian jazz pianist and singer Monique diMattina says* …: Monique diMattina, 'In the mind's ear', *Dumbo Feather*, November 2020, no. 65, dumbofeather.com/articles/in-the-minds-ear.

page 229 *Author Charlotte Wood envisages a circus tent …*: Charlotte Wood, *The Luminous Solution: Creativity, Resilience and the Inner Life*, Allen & Unwin, Sydney, 2021.

page 230 *It's this exposure to and immersion in the natural environment …*: Matt P. Stevenson, Theresa Schilhab & Peter Bentsen, 'Attention Restoration Theory II: a systematic review to clarify attention processes affected by exposure to natural environments', *Journal of Toxicology and Environmental Health Part B: Critical Reviews*, 2018, vol. 21, no. 4, pp. 227–68, doi.org/10.1080/10937404.2018.1505571.

page 230 *For writer Maggie MacKellar …*: Maggie MacKellar, 'Something beginning with E', The Sit Spot, 13 August 2024, maggiemackellar.substack.com/p/something-beginning-with-e.

page 230 *Author Hilde Hinton builds …*: Irma Gold & Karen Viggers, 'Hilde Hinton', *Secrets from the Green Room* (podcast), season 5, episode 47, podcasts.apple.com/au/podcast/secrets-from-the-green-room/id1540540062.

page 231 *'I've been at this long enough to know …'*: Abigail Thomas, *Still Life at Eighty: The Next Interesting Thing*, Scribner, New York, 2024.

page 231 *Garner admits that interest is enough …*: Jake Niall, '"I thought, geez, this is a happy story": Helen Garner on her footy book', *Sydney Morning Herald*, 23 November 2024, smh.com.au/culture/books/i-thought-geez-this-is-a-happy-story-helen-garner-on-her-footy-book-20241119-p5krxd.html.

page 234 *Psychologists believe slow looking is one key …*: Antonio Crego, José Ramón Yela, María Ángeles Gómez-Martínez et al., 'Relationships between mindfulness, purpose in life, happiness, anxiety, and depression: testing a mediation model in a sample of women', *International Journal of Environmental Research and Public Health*, 2021, vol. 18, no. 3, pp. 1–15, doi.org/10.3390/ijerph18030925.

page 234 *Science also tells us that this questioning …*: Matthias J. Gruber & Charan Ranganath, 'How curiosity enhances hippocampus-dependent memory: the Prediction, Appraisal, Curiosity, and Exploration (PACE) framework', *Trends in Cognitive Sciences*, 2019, vol. 23, no. 12, pp. 1014–25, doi.org/10.1016/j.tics.2019.10.003.

page 234 *Charlotte Wood, in her book …*: Charlotte Wood, *The Luminous Solution: Creativity, Resilience and the Inner Life*, Allen & Unwin, Sydney, 2021.

page 234 *this premise … increases the neural activity in the brain circuits …*: Matthias J. Gruber, Barnard D. Gelman, Charan Ranganath, 'States of curiosity modulate hippocampus-dependent learning via the dopaminergic circuit', *Neuron*, 2014, vol. 84, no. 2, pp. 486–96, doi.org/10.1016/j.neuron.2014.08.060.

page 234 *And while curiosity is vital … research shows that it's essential for adults …*: Shannon McGillivray, Kou Murayama & Alan D. Castel, 'Thirst for knowledge: the effects of curiosity and interest on memory in younger and older adults', *Psychology and Aging*, 2015, vol. 30, no. 4, pp. 835–41, doi.org/10.1037/a0039801.

page 237 *Biologist Edward O. Wilson developed the biophilia hypothesis …*: Edward O. Wilson, *Biophilia*, Harvard University Press, Boston, Massachusetts, 1984.

page 238 *spending time in nature improves health … stress levels decrease*: Michelle C. Kondo, Sara F. Jacoby & Eugenia C. South, 'Does spending time outdoors reduce stress? A review of real-time stress response to outdoor environments', *Health and Place*, 2018, vol. 51, pp. 136–50, doi.org/10.1016/j.healthplace.2018.03.001.

page 238 *But the science supports what our bodies have always told us …*: Mathew P. White, Ian Alcock, James Grellier et al., 'Spending at least 120 minutes a week in nature is associated with good health and wellbeing', *Scientific Reports*, 2019, vol. 9, article no. 7730, doi.org/10.1038/s41598-019-44097-3.

pages 238–39 *Even a short walk in a city park can affect …*: Simone Kühn, Anna Mascherek, Elisa Filevich et al., 'Spend time outdoors for your brain: an in-depth longitudinal MRI study', *World Journal of Biological Psychiatry*, 2022, vol. 23, no. 3, pp. 201–207, doi.org/10.1080/15622975.2021.1938670.

page 243 *As writer and mother Kerri ní Dochartaigh says …*: Kerri ní Dochartaigh, *Thin Places*, Canongate, London, 2021.

Conclusion

page 245 *Stepping into open space fosters our curiosity …*: Maison Abu Raya, Adedoyin O. Ogunyemi, Jake Broder et al., 'The neurobiology of openness as a personality trait', *Frontiers in Neurology*, 2023, vol. 14, article no. 1235345, doi.org/10.3389/fneur.2023.1235345.

page 247 *Author Annie Dillard considers habits …*: Annie Dillard, *The Writing Life*, Harper & Row, New York, 1989.

Epilogue

page 252 *As my teacher …*: Charlotte Wood, *The Luminous Solution: Creativity, Resilience and the Inner Life*, Allen & Unwin, Sydney, 2021.

acknowledgements

Some books come along just when you need to read them. This book came along just when I needed to write it.

To Alexandra Payne who initially commissioned me, thank you. It was perfect timing.

Justin Wolfers, thank you for caring deeply, throwing yourself into the manuscript and taking it further than I could alone. I hope every writer experiences the immense joy of working with a publisher like you.

I count myself incredibly lucky to be a part of the Murdoch Books team who have supported me since 2020, but special thanks, always, to Jane Morrow, for your creative clarity and pragmatic advice.

Thanks to my exemplary editing team – Loran McDougall and Nicola Young – and to my publicist, Sue Bobbermein, who does the vital work of getting my books into the right hands.

When I set out to better understand my brain, I looked to science to help me make sense of my biology. This book wouldn't exist without the generous experts who gave their time and shared their knowledge with me: Lara Bertolino, Jack Feldman, Ann-Christine Duhaime, Damian Holsinger, Avik Basu, Gordon Parker, Madeleine Murray and Allison Davies.

Special thanks also to the people who shared their intimate understanding of the world: Jane Hilliard, Heather Plett, Rebecca Hooper, Alex Boon, Natalie Mendham, Robyn Thomas, Judith Abell, Michelle Wild, Megan Walch and Koren Helbig.

To Charlotte Wood and the Ten Experiments crew, who have bolstered my writing life since 2024, a heartfelt and very gracious thank you.

To my librarian, Lyn, thank you for your ongoing support, and thanks to the Libraries Tasmania and the Open Libraries program, which offers meaningful creative arts support in the form of a quiet space for me to write every day of the week.

Thank you to my partner, Daniel, and my children – Che, Poet, Percy and Marigold – who cheer and celebrate me in all the ways that matter.

And to Sandy, for the persistent nudges, salty beach walks and cherished companionship.

about the author

Jodi Wilson is a bestselling author, health journalist, yoga teacher and postpartum doula. Her previous books include *Practising Simplicity* and the number-one-selling *The Complete Australian Guide to Pregnancy and Birth* and *The Complete Guide to Postpartum*. Her work has been published by *The Guardian* and the ABC, and she writes two weekly newsletters on Substack – *Practising Simplicity* and *Dear New Mum*. She lives in a small town in Lutruwita/ Tasmania with her partner and their four children.